The Most Tenacious of Minorities
The Jews of Italy

The Most Tenacious of Minorities

The Jews of Italy

SARA REGUER

Boston
2013

Library of Congress Cataloging-in-Publication Data:
A catalog record for this book as available from the Library of Congress.

ISBN 978-1-64469-030-7
Book design by Ivan Grave
On the cover: Map of Italy. Mapmaker: J. Bludell, London 1720.

Published by Academic Studies Press in 2013
28 Montfern Avenue
Brighton, MA 02135, USA
press@academicstudiespress.com
www.academicstudiespress.com

To Raffaele Gershom Fodde

Anna-Alexandra Fodde-Reguer   *Elizabeth Ruth Fodde-Reguer*

ACKNOWLEDGEMENTS

My interest in the Jews of Italy began in earnest when I married an Italian Jew. What started as a peripheral interest, deepened as I created an undergraduate course on "Italian Jewry" at Brooklyn College. At my students' urging, and with the support of my family, I then embarked on writing a user-friendly book that could be used in the classroom as well as by the interested public.

I acknowledge the support given to me by the PSC/CUNY grant [1997], the Brine Family Trust grant [2008, and the Tow Travel Grant of Brooklyn College [2009]. I am grateful for the assistance of Shulamith Berger, Curator of special Collections of Yeshiva University, and for the cooperation of the library at the Jewish Theological Seminary of America, the Palatina Library of Parma, as well as the museum at Aquileia.

Kyle Goen helped with the maps, Elizabeth Fodde-Reguer helped with preparing the physical manuscript, and Anna Fodde-Reguer helped with the preliminary editing. I thank my colleagues at the Department of Judaic Studies at Brooklyn College—Jonathan Helfand, Sharon Flatto, and Robert Shapiro—for their encouragement to keep going.

To my husband Raffaele Fodde this book is dedicated in recognition of the profound debt that I owe him in helping this book come into being. His linguistic skills and breadth of knowledge constantly amaze me. It is also dedicated to my two daughters, Anna-Alexandra and Elizabeth Ruth, whose mantra was always, "You can do it!"

Contents

PREFACE

I am often asked how I got interested in Italian Jewish history. The simple answer is: I married an Italian Jew. What started off as an interest in differences and similarities in religious customs expanded into a fascination with Italian synagogue architecture and ritual objects and books, and I gradually found myself looking at the "Italian" take on the specific time division of Jewish history. I had noticed, but not really paid attention to, the remarkable number of Italian authors who appear in the prayer book. Having visited Rome as a college student, I knew of the Arch of Titus and the enslavement of the rebellious Jews of Israel, but never really asked about the Jewish community already in Rome at the time of the destruction of the Second Temple.

As a result of my gradually expanding interest, I decided to teach a course on Italian Jewry, knowing that this step would force me to both organize my disconnected reading and search out as much primary source material as I could find. Doing so was a major learning experience for me, and in refining the course over the years, as well as doing research in specific areas that connected to my interests in Middle Eastern Jewish history, Sephardic history, and women's history, I developed the idea for this book.

I am a strong believer in putting the history of a minority group into the larger context, which is in this case both Italian history and mainstream Jewish history. Italian Jews were Jews as well as Italians. If Italian history and culture is unique, then this created a unique minority group that had characteristics specific to Italy. Jewish history is a history of re-creation of community, and I will attempt to describe how this came about in Italy. The

Jews arrived in what we now call Italy from Greek-speaking Alexandria and later Byzantium, and from Aramaic-speaking Judea and Iraq. They were later joined by German and Provençal speakers coming from the north, Arabic speakers from the south, and Spanish speakers from Iberia. Except for the earliest groups, Jews arrived in already existing communities which accepted them as fellow Jews, but at the same time both the new arrivals and the members of the existing communities recognized that there were differences. Some of these differences disappeared over the centuries, but others did not, and so we have splinter groups within what was already a small minority. The basic glue holding them together was Judaism. This is true today as well, as Jews moved to Italy from Libya, Lebanon, Iran, and the former Soviet Union. The difference is that now we can witness the re-creation of their communities and their Italianization.

Timeline

GENERAL		JEWISH
Egyptian Kingdom	c. 1280	Exodus from Egypt
Philistines settle the coast of Canaan	c. 1250	Joshua
	c. 1020—1000	Rule of Saul
	c. 1000—961	Rule of David
	961—922	Rule of Solomon
Rise of Assyria	745 721	Fall of 10 northern tribes of Israel
Rise of Babylon	612	
Nebuchadnezzar	605—562	
	597	Yehoyachin and aristocracy exiled to Babylon
	587/6	Fall of Jerusalem, start of Babylonian Exile
Rise of Persia	539	
	538—332	Second Commonwealth under Persia
	516	Second Temple
Roman Republic	509—44	
Alexander the Great / Greece Conquest of Middle East	332	
	332—190	Second Commonwealth under Greeks / Ptolemeys / Seleucids
Ptolemeys rule Palestine	301—200	
Seleucids rule Palestine	200—168	
	168	Judah Maccabee leads rebellion
Rome and Judea	161	Treaty between Judah and Rome
	160—63	Independent Hasmonean dynasty
Rome conquers Judea	63 BCE	
	63 BCE—70 CE	Second Commonwealth under Rome
Julius Caesar assassinated	44 BCE	
Rome crushes Judean Rebellion	70 CE	Destruction of Second Temple

Chapter 1

EARLY BEGINNINGS

Jewish history begins in the Land of Israel during the Biblical period. The experiences of the three generations of the Patriarchs and Matriarchs, the descent of their children to Egypt, their Exodus hundreds of years later led by Moses, the Covenant at Sinai, the entry into the land of Israel and its gradual conquest, and the monarchs and prophets are described in the *Tanakh*, the Hebrew Bible. These writings end with the destruction of the First Temple, in 586 BCE, and the Babylonian Exile. The period of the Second Commonwealth has three stages: the Persian (536—334 BCE), the Greek (334-63 BCE), and the Roman (63BCE—70 CE).

The center of Jewish life during the Persian period, emotionally if not numerically, continued to be the land of Israel. The population center, however, was Babylon, and trade routes brought Jews to the far reaches of the Persian Empire. Gradually, after the Persian authorities allowed the Jews to return and rebuild the western provinces of Judea, Samaria, and Galilee, the demographics changed somewhat, particularly when the new Temple in Jerusalem was erected and the Temple service re-established.

However, the exclusive Temple-centered religion of the earlier period was not recreated. One of the survival tactics created in Babylon was the development of the forerunner of the modern synagogue. Judaism proved to be the one ancient religion that, although originally geographically centered on its

> **Psalm 137, 1-6**
>
> By the rivers of Babylon,
> There we sat and wept,
> As we thought of Zion.
> There on the poplars
> We hung up our lyres
> For our captors asked us for songs,
> Our tormentors, for amusement
> "Sing us a song of Zion."
> How can we sing a song of the Lord
> On alien soil?
> If I forget thee, O Jerusalem,
> Let my right hand wither.
> Let my tongue stick to my palate
> If I cease to think of thee,
> If I do not keep Jerusalem in memory
> Even in my happiest hour.

land of origin and its holy sites there, was resilient after its uprooting. After bewailing the loss of their independence and their enslavement, the Judeans in Babylon probably began to meet informally on Sabbaths and holidays. What was done at these gatherings is only guesswork, but Torah scrolls were definitely available, as presumably were other books of the *Tanakh*, which was not yet complete. Sages and priests knew how to formulate the calendar, and the earlier exile of their aristocracy provided them with some leadership already in place. By the time the Persians defeated the Babylonians, the idea of a synagogue—a *Bet Knesset* or house of gathering— was in place. Traveling Jews would have spread these new ideas to other communities.

Therefore, when the Persians allowed the Jews to return to Judea and rebuild the Temple in Jerusalem, the returnees brought with them the new institution of *Bet Knesset,* and such buildings co-existed with the Temple. There probably was one in every city in Judea, Samaria, and the Galilee, in addition to those in the cities of the diaspora. The synagogue also contributed to the growing importance of the scribe-scholar, who competed with the priests for the religious leadership of the people.

One thing that had changed completely between the time of the first Temple and that of the second was the tribal structure of the people. The "Israelites," divided into the twelve tribes of antiquity, became the "Jews," whose name was based on the only large tribe to survive exile intact, the tribe of Judah. Any members of the other tribes who had survived had merged with the Judeans. But the returning Jews divided themselves in other ways: one was defined by the

---

Decree of Cyrus the Great, king of Persia 559-529 BCE, in Ezra 1, 1-4

In the first year of King Cyrus of Persia, when the word of the Lord spoken by Jeremiah was fulfilled, the Lord roused the spirit of King Cyrus of Persia to issue a proclamation throughout his realm by word of mouth and in writing as follows: "Thus said King Cyrus of Persia: The Lord God of Heaven has given me all the kingdoms of the earth and has charged me with building Him a house in Jerusalem, which is in Judah. Any one of you of all His people—may his God be with him, and let him go up to Jerusalem that is in Judah and build the House of the Lord God of Israel, the God that is in Jerusalem; and all who stay behind, wherever he may be living, let the people of his place assist him with silver, gold, goods, and livestock, besides the freewill offering to the House of God that is in Jerusalem."

---

distinctions placed between the Cohen (priest), the Levite, and Israelite, distinctions centered on Temple ritual, which eventually left their traces mainly in synagogue worship. Another division was that of class: there was a small aristocracy at the top, which included wealthy Jews, then a middle class of petty traders and merchants, and finally a large lower class consisting of farmers, herdsmen, and craftspeople. At the very bottom of society were the slaves. One last division, which is in keeping with most societies of the time, was that of gender.

The family continued to be the basic building block of Jewish society. It continued to be patriarchal, with the oldest male at the head of the family making the important decisions relating to his domain. Women also made decisions, but their world was more complex, and matriarchal rights depended on a woman's position in the family. The family was also patrilocal, in that when a couple married, the woman usually moved into the household of her husband, and patrilinial, with one's ancestry usually traced on the male side. The family was also an extended one, with multiple generations living together and each member knowing his or her place in the pecking order. People married within the family if possible, for an endogamous marriage protected the wealth of the family: *mohar,* or brideswealth had to be paid by the groom's side of the family to the bride's side. Such a marriage also ensured the status of the bride and protected her, for her mother-in-law was usually her aunt or cousin, rather than a stranger. First marriages were arranged by family patriarchs or their representatives, and the young people usually had little say. Families were also polygynous, with men who could afford it marrying more than one wife. It is within this context that women's rights were delimited, for her rights differed depending on whether she was a primary wife, a secondary wife, or a concubine. The primary wife obviously had the most power, and she usually ran the women's part of the family structure; her children were guaranteed to inherit the patriarch's wealth.

The Jewish family structure reflected that of general Middle Eastern society at the time, but did not copy it exactly, for Judaism colored every aspect of life including the family structure. For example, religion determined exactly which relatives one could marry and which ones were forbidden.

One aspect of the extended family concept, which in its widest context was part of clan identity, was the idea of helping one's "own." Thus, when

Biblical Verses on Charity

He shall not dominate with harshness over him [the Hebrew slave]. Lev. 25:53

A stranger you shall not wrong nor oppress, for you were a stranger in Egypt. Exod. 22:20

You shall not afflict a widow nor an orphan. Exod.22:21

You shall not be to him [a needy man] as a demanding creditor. Exod. 22:24

You shall not wholly reap the corner of your field. Neither shall you gather the gleanings of your harvest. And you shall not glean your vineyard.... You shall leave them for the poor and the stranger. Lev. 19:9-10

You shall not harden your heart, but you shall surely open wide your hand to him. Deut. 15:7-8

You shall not go back to fetch it ... it shall be for the stranger, the orphan, and the widow. Deut. 24:19

a member of a family was in need, other members came to assist him or her. The laws of Judaism extended this by spelling out specific types of charity. For example, one that was quite important for a people anchored in agriculture, the owner of a field had to leave the corners of the field to be harvested by the poor. Additionally, any grains that fell to the ground during the reaping of the field could not be retrieved, but were also left to the poor. In other words, the idea of charity was imprinted on the early Israelites, and this concept was taken with them into Babylon and onward, into whatever places the Jews later found themselves. One of the more important acts of charity, if one could compare them, was considered to be the redemption of captives. However, this was an expensive undertaking, and it quickly became the responsibility of group effort, centered in the synagogues.

A constant in the lives of the Jews was religious belief. Traditional Jews believe that both the written law and its oral interpretation were handed down to Moses on Mount Sinai. The chain of tradition that followed Moses was Joshua, the Elders, the prophets, and, after prophecy ended, the men of the *Knesset ha-Gedolah* (the Great Assembly).

Oral tradition was referred to as *halakha* (the path), and it encompassed every aspect of life, from making offerings in the Temple to keeping laws of the Sabbath and holidays, from engaging in

Tractate *Avot, mishna* 1

Moses received the Law on Sinai and gave it over to Joshua, and Joshua to the Elders, and the Elders to the Prophets, and the Prophets gave it over to the men of the Great Knesset. They said three things: be deliberate in judgment, teach many disciples, and make a fence around the Law.

marital relations to upholding criminal law and social order. *Halakha* was based mainly on interpretation of the Biblical text, and over time a set of logical rules was laid out. However, *halakha* was never static, and as new situations arose which presented new dilemmas, the interpreters of Jewish law found logical answers through methods like precedent or analogy. If these methods did not work, they emended the law. Added to this was the development over time of customs, which were not specifically anchored in Biblical commandments.

The study of Torah became part of Jewish life during the Second Temple period, and it became customary to teach children to read as well as study the rules of Judaism. The most talented students could earn the title of *hakham*, "sage," and it was these sages who both interpreted law and taught it. Various sages gathered around themselves students who participated in intellectual discussion, the most talented of whom would later "inherit" their teachers' informal schools.

It would be an error to assume that the Jews were a monochromatic people, for they held a variety of opinions and so religious life even in Second Temple Israel was complex and sometimes controversial. One complicating factor was the competing Babylonian center, which, while aware of intellectual developments in Jerusalem and the surrounding cities, developed its own sages and made its own legal decisions. This was especially complex when political borders made travel between Israel and Babylon difficult, such as when the Ptolemeys ruled Israel (301-200 BCE) and the Seleucids repeatedly attempted to conquer it. The focus of the *halakhic* discussion in Babylon was geared more to the realities of the diaspora, and thus not much attention was paid, for example, to agricultural laws that only affected the land of Israel, or that focused on Temple ritual and purity. There was also intense Jewish sectarianism in the late Second Temple period, which affected some of the legal decisions.

No matter where Jews lived, they viewed Jerusalem as their spiritual center, for it was the locus of the Temple and the birthplace of their identity. They not only faced Jerusalem as they prayed—for prayer was developing and replacing the traditional offerings, which could only take place in the Temple itself—but they also sent money to pay for its upkeep, specifically the half-shekel required by Jewish law. Diaspora Jews were aware of *halakhic* decisions, and we presume that some of the sages' students traveled to diaspora communities. News traveled along trade routes, and religious pilgrims who went to the Temple in Jerusalem to celebrate festivals also added to the awareness of new developments.

Central to the re-creation of Jewish communities all over the Middle East and North Africa was the building of synagogues, which functioned as both places of prayer and meeting places. The idea of the synagogue was brought to the northern Mediterranean lands under Greek rule. Alexander the Great defeated the Persian Empire in approximately 334 BCE, and this led to this expansion of Jewish communities westward along the North African coast. Egypt, with the founding of Alexandria, was especially popular, despite the memory of Pharaonic enslavement, for the Jews were attracted to imperial centers with their economic possibilities. After Alexander's death and the division of his empire into three parts, under three dynasties, most of the Jews ended up under either Seleucus I—who obtained Syria, Mesopotamia, and Iran—or Ptolemy I—who obtained Egypt and Judea.

Many of the Jews attracted to Alexandria gradually became Hellenized. It is probable that the *Tanakh*, which by then had been more or less finalized by the sages in Jerusalem, was translated into Greek for them by a group of Alexandrian scholars, and the *Septuagint*, as this translation was known, included not only the sacred texts known as the Torah, Prophets, and Writings, but also the "External Books," better known by the Greek term *Apocrypha*, which were written between 285 and 244 BCE. Using this translation was a practical response to the lack of traditional Hebrew education, and an important effect of the use of the Greek language was that it made the texts available to the lower classes as well. The Jewish Bible was thereby prevented from becoming the exclusive property of the priests, sages, and scribes. The translation also enabled the general Greek-speaking public to read the sacred works, thereby attracting converts. When these Greek-speaking Jews moved to the northern Mediterranean cities, they took the *Septuagint* with them as they began to replant communities on the

> **Legend of the Septuagint, Tractate *Megilla* 9**
>
> King Ptolemey [3d century BCE] once gathered seventy-two elders. He placed them in seventy-two chambers, each of them in a separate one, without revealing to them why they were summoned. He entered each one's room and said: "Write for me the Torah of Moshe, your teacher." God put it in the heart of each one to translate identically as all the others did.

Italian peninsula. It is natural for immigrants to try to replant what they are accustomed to, but for Jews it was vital not just to replant, but to re-create their religious and community structures, without which they could disappear as a unique people.

Why did some Jews move to the Italian peninsula? During the long history of the Jewish people, the decision of individuals to move has usually been based on a combination of push-pull effects. The most obvious "push" reason to move was that of safety. Religious persecution in the home country, or even the threat of it, was a major push. Fear of war in the home country, or war actually breaking out, was another. Sometimes the move was made without any choice, for example, when Jews were enslaved. But often it was the "pull" effect of economics that tilted the scale in the decision to move. The home country might have been suffering from a drought or a series of bad crops, or individuals might have felt that there was little possibility of advancing economically. But it was also the stories passed on by travelers, describing other areas as doing well, that played a part in the decision to move, and Rome was rapidly becoming an economic lodestone.

Italian culture was so different from other Mediterranean cultures in part because of the specific qualities of the Etruscans whose civilization lasted from about the tenth century BCE until it fell to the Latin and Sabine tribes in about the year 400 BCE. These 600 years of Etruscan rule laid the groundwork for a culture that stressed an individualistic life geared to happiness, music, merriment, and enjoyment of good things. The Etruscans were scientific farmers and excellent seamen, and when they conquered Rome in about 600 BCE, they transformed it from a primitive village into a great city. However, they were not a nation but rather a group of city-states with separate dialects and no discipline nor organization. It was therefore no surprise that the Etruscans fell to the tribal groups of Latins and Sabines, who then turned southward from Rome to conquer the Greek-controlled south.

The Greeks had entered Sicily in the eighth century BCE, moving northward as far as Naples. It is said that they introduced the olive tree and the grapevine into Italy. Just as important was that they brought in the basics of Western civilization. Their enmity with Carthage, a power that had started as a colony of Phoenicia, was replaced by a similar rivalry with the Romans, who, by the third century BCE, were expanding southward. The Roman Republic, founded in 509 BCE, manifested from the beginning the Romans' talents as both organizers and administrators. The gradual development of law was accompanied by the concept of citizenship, which at first was only for free males of the original three tribes of Rome, but was gradually extended to include free slaves and aliens. Citizens enjoyed many immunities and had the right to appeal to the Assembly. Power lay in the hands of the two consuls, who had equal power and were elected for one year, and they were advised by a 300-member Senate. Society was divided into a patrician class, "equites" or well-to-do businessmen, plebes or the common people, which included peasants and workers, and, at the bottom, slaves. It is within this context that the Jews moved to the Italian peninsula.

The two types of Jews who ended up in Italy were from opposite ends of the economic strata: sons of international traders would be sent to set up new outposts for the family trade, and lower-class craftsmen would arrive plying their talents. If the migration pattern followed the historical norm for Jews, the initial immigrants were usually male, but once they had made some money they would send for their wives and children. The majority of Jews who came to Rome in these early stages were of the lower class group. This was the 'pull' reason for the move.

It may have been this community that informed the Jews in the land of Israel of the rising Roman power, which then led to political actions on Judea's part. When the Seleucids took control of Judea in 198 BCE, their ruler, Antiochus III, initially allowed the Jews to continue as a semiautonomous group. But when Antiochus IV Epiphanes (175-163 BCE) took over, things changed drastically. He was not only interested in the Temple in Jerusalem for its treasure, he was also interested in unifying his people, probably in part for idealistic reasons, but certainly in part from a practical perspective: a unified people would be better able to withstand any external force. He embarked on a policy of enforced hellenization, which led to the Maccabean revolt in Judea. It is this revolt that led to the first Jewish document connecting the Jews of the land of Israel with the Romans, the *Book of Maccabees*, one of the books of the *Apocrypha*. The Maccabees, intent on wresting back their independence from the Seleucid Greeks, wanted an ally and found it in the Roman Republic. The *Book of Maccabees* attests to a mutual aid pact between the Hasmonean dynasty and the Roman Republic. But because there is no Roman source to back this up, some scholars claim that it never occurred. According to 1 *Maccabees* 8, Judah had heard about the Romans:

They were renowned for their military power and for the welcome they gave to those who became their allies; any who joined them could be sure of their firm friendship. He was told about the wars they had fought, and the valour they had shown in their conquest of the Gauls, whom they had laid under tribute. He heard of their successes in Spain, where they had seized silver-mines and gold-mines.... There were kings from far and near who had marched against them, but they had been beaten off after crushing defeats; others paid them annual tribute.... For all of this, not one of them made any personal claim to greatness by wearing the crown or donning the purple. They had established a senate where 320 [sic] senators met daily to deliberate, giving constant thought to the proper ordering of the affairs of the common people. They entrusted their government and the ruling of all their territory to one [sic] of their number every year, all obeying this one man without envy or jealousy among themselves.

So Judah appointed a delegation of two men to go to Rome to conclude a treaty of friendship and alliance to help them fight off the Greek Seleucids. The Romans in the Senate heard the request and replied in the affirmative, inscribing the treaty on tablets of bronze, which were sent to Jerusalem.

Success to the Romans and the Jewish nation by sea and land for ever! May sword and foe be far from them! But if war breaks out first against Rome ... then the Jewish nation shall support them.... Similarly, if war breaks out first against the Jewish nation, then the Roman shall give them such hearty support as the occasion may require.... These are the terms of the agreement which the Romans have made with the Jewish people. But if, hereafter, both parties shall agree to add or to rescind anything, then they shall do as they decide; any such addition or rescindment shall be valid.

Whether this treaty was in fact made or not, the information provided shows how aware the Hasmoneans were of the Roman Republic. We will soon move into verifiable material with the reign of Julius Caesar.

The stage is now set for the growth and development of what would become a unique Jewish community, the most tenacious minority in Europe: namely, the Jews of Italy.

Recommended Reading

Baron, Salo W. *A Social and Religious History of the Jews*. Philadelphia: JPS, 1952-83. 18 volumes.

Cohen, Shaye. *From the Maccabees to the Mishnah*. Philadelphia: Westminster Press, 1987.

Schwartz, Leo. *Great Ages and Ideas of the Jewish People*. New York: Random House, 1956.

Stern, M. "The Period of the Second Temple." In *A History of the Jewish People*, ed. H.H. Ben-Sasson. London: Wiedenfeld and Nicolson, 1976.

Chapter 2

ROMAN RULE

In the year 63 BCE, Pompey made Judea a province of the Roman Republic after killing many Jews, violating the Temple in Jerusalem, and enslaving Jewish nobles, forcing them to march in his triumphal procession in Rome. The Hasmonean dynasty was limping to its conclusion. It stood to reason, therefore, that during the showdown between Pompey and Caesar over who should lead the Republic, the Jews of both Judea and Egypt backed Julius Caesar. Caesar, therefore had a personal reason for dealing well with the Jews. He was also a prime example of the Roman idealist, who tolerated all national customs.

Before addressing what Julius Caesar did for the Jews, we have to address the questions of where the Jews came from. What do we know about them at this early period, and how do we know it?

Timeline

GENERAL		JEWISH
Roman Republic	509—44 BCE	Alexandrian Jews arrive in Rome
Julius Caesar	100—44 BCE	Regulations affecting Jews
Rule of Augustus Caesar	31 BCE—14 CE	
Rule of Tiberius	14—37 CE	
	19 CE	4,000 Jews exiled to Sardinia
Beginning and spread of Christianity	First Century CE	
	66	Judean Rebellion
	37—c. 100	Life of Josephus
Arch of Titus built	70	Second Temple destroyed—Yavneh Academy founded
	70—c. 361	*Fiscus Judaicus*
	95	Palestinian deputation
	132—135	Bar Kokhba Revolt
	c. 200	Mishna redacted
Persian (Sassanid) Empire	226—632	
Edict of Milan	313	
Rule of Constantine	324—337	
Split between Western and Eastern Roman Empires	395	
	c. 400	Palestinian Talmud redacted
	429	End of Palestinian Academy
Theodosian Codex	438	
	c. 500	Babylonian Talmud redacted
Justinian Code	528	
Pope Gregory I	590—604	
Arab armies begin to invade Middle East	632	

The Jews came from two main centers, namely Egypt, where the city of Alexandria had an important and sizeable Jewish population, and the land of Israel, from which they arrived as either freemen or war prisoners. Most of them settled in the city of Rome, across the Tiber River, in the neighborhood known as Trastevere. Other Jews settled in cities known for trade, for example in Pozzuoli (near Naples), Brindisi, and Pompeii, to the south of Rome itself. Another center of Jewish life was in the northeastern Roman garrison city of Aquilaea, where Jews, along with their co-religionists in Trastevere, introduced glassmaking to Europe. The class society of Rome at first contained no Jews who could be considered patricians, as most were common people involved in petty trade and crafts. Those who arrived as war prisoners did not long remain as such, for the free Jews of Rome were very much aware of the injunction of freeing fellow Jews from slavery. Some of these Roman Jews were more middle class, owning small businesses. In a society that had little interest in commerce and whose members were focused on a *latifundia*, or feudal land system with slaves working the soil, the Jews were able to carve out niches for themselves.

What kind of city was Rome at that time? It was a city built by the master engineers of antiquity. It was a city with paved streets, some of which are still used today; it was a city with aquaducts and viaducts to bring water to an ever-growing population; it was a city with a sewage system. Indeed, Rome had a form of flush toilets, a convenience which did not reach London until the time of Queen Victoria. A city with these amenities could easily grow to house a population of 300,000, within a population of about 1.3 million in the entire city-state. The number of Jews residing in Rome in this era is a matter of disagreement, and the figure given ranges from 12,000 to 40,000.

Some primary sources giving us information about the Roman Jews are the stone slabs, either painted or incised, that have been found in the Jewish underground cemeteries or catacombs. The Romans did not bury their dead but burned them. Tacitus, the Roman historian, considered the Jews to be barbarians for burying their dead, but this was a custom dating back to the Biblical Patriarchs. How can one tell that these were Jewish catacombs and not those of another minority community? Normally, one would look for Hebrew lettering or Jewish symbols such as the Star of David. But the latter was not used by Jews at this time, and the Jews carved the several hundred epitaphs, or inscriptions, on their burial plaques, in Greek

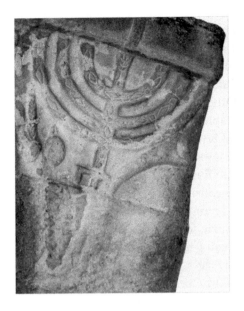

Close up of stone relief from architrave
of Ostia synagogue, with symbols
of menorah, lulav, etrog, and shofar.
Ostia was the port city of ancient Rome
(Photograph, R. Fodde collection)

and Latin, with the earliest stones carved in Greek and the later ones in a combination of Greek and Latin. Only some contained a word or two of Hebrew. As for the symbols which were painted or carved on the plaques, they include the seven-branched candelabrum or *menorah* (symbolic of the *menorah* of the Temple), a citron and a palm branch or *lulav* (symbolic of the holiday of Succot), and a *shofar* or ram's horn (symbolic of the holiday of *Rosh ha-Shana*). Some symbols are artistically crude, while others are of the highest order, probably attesting to differences in wealth among the deceased. Some attest to the status of the deceased as a freedman, while others attest to more humble crafts.

These burial plaques, as well as other primary sources, like legal documents, many of which were Roman, point to the probability that the diaspora communities of the Greco-Roman world used Greek in writing and speech, even in the synagogue. The Torah portion was read in Hebrew with Greek translation, probably by chanting first the Hebrew verse, followed by its Greek translation. It is possible, however, that it was read exclusively in Greek in the initial stages of settlement. The community was organized in the style of the Greek *polis*, to which the titles of the office-holders attest. This was unlike what we know of the Jewish community structure in Babylon, where much more Hebrew was used.

Early Jewish tombstone, Latin inscription, Jewish symbol of the menorah. Encased in the wall of the basilica of Milan (Photograph, R. Fodde collection)

The freedom to worship was possible because of Julius Caesar, who safeguarded Jewish interests via regulations. Jewish representatives could and did petition Roman rulers as they had petitioned the Roman Senate, and four of the regulations Caesar enacted give us important insights into the Roman Jewish community. First, the Jews did not have to do military service which could jeopardize religious observances. This first regulation probably reflects the Jewish laws of the Sabbath, as well as those regarding keeping kosher; we therefore presume that this community continued to strictly observe these laws, which are basic to Judaism.

A second regula-tion was that Jews could judge their own cases using Jewish law. This is a little more complicated, for it did not mean that Jews could break Roman law. It presumes that the cases involved Jew versus Jew rather than Jew versus Roman. Again, this points to the reality of Jewish diaspora life: the Jews lived Jewish neighborhoods and mixed mainly with fellow Jews, so contacts with non-Jews would be limited to business and trade. It was normal for members of minority groups, whether religious or ethnic, to live in the same area; this was even more so the case for Jews. Jews needed to have easy access to kosher food, for example, and in a society that had no refrigeration animals had to be slaughtered, butchered, and cooked as quickly as possible. They also needed to be close to the *scuola* from the Latin word for synagogue, *schola*, for daily prayer services. Further, the comfort level of living among one's own group is important. This regulation also points to the likelihood that the Jews had expanded the functions of the synagogue beyond those of house of prayer and house of study; it also functioned as a *bet din* or religious court. This finding fits with the fact that such buildings were used this way in even older Jewish communities in the ancient world.

A third regulation passed by Julius Caesar was one exempting the synagogue, the *scuola*, from the general Roman ban on "associations," or public meetings of three or more men. The Roman law was geared to preventing sedition and rebellion, and Caesar understood that gatherings of Jews were for reasons of prayer to their unseen God and study of the sacred scriptures. Again, this can be interpreted as a proof text demonstrating that one of the first signs of the re-creation of Jewish communities is the establishment of a house of prayer, which also serves as a house of learning, and, at times, as a religious court. There are numerous archeological finds that underscore the importance of the establishment of the *scuola*, some only recently uncovered. Ostia, the harbor of ancient Rome, provides us with the best example of ancient Roman synagogues. For a long time, it was surmised that certain buildings found were regular pagan temples, but with the realization that all of them were faced eastward toward Jerusalem, and that the wall and pillar decorations included seven-branched candelabra, scholars adjusted their findings and concluded that they were ancient synagogues. One decoration attests to the fact that the holy ark, placed in the front of the synagogue, housed individual scrolls, probably one for each of the Five Books of the Torah, which were stored in pigeonhole-like cubicles rather than in a standing position. By the third century CE, there were probably eleven synagogues in Rome itself, but they functioned independent of one another, without an umbrella organization such as the Alexandrian community had. Each had its own officers and dignitaries, bearing titles such as *archisynagogus*, which seems to have designated the leader, combining the functions of president and rabbi, and even representing the community to the Roman powers. The *archisynagogus* had assistants with their own titles, including one in charge of the services and one in charge of the finances.

The final of these four regulations stated that the Jews could send money to the Temple in Jerusalem. This was the one exception to the Roman rule against exporting gold and wealth out of the Republic. Jewish men between the ages of 18 and about 50 were required to pay an annual half shekel for the upkeep of the Temple. This tie to both the homeland and the central focus of Jewish worship kept the diaspora Jews feeling connected to the religious heartland. The relationship was a reciprocal one: money was sent from Italy, and eventually visits were paid by Palestine center representatives to the diaspora community in Rome.

After the assassination of Julius Caesar, in 44 BCE, the Republic of Rome died. A triumvirate took over, with Anthony ruling the east, Octavian the west, and Lepidus ruling Carthage in North Africa. It was only a matter of time before Octavian began amassing greater power into his own hands, becoming the first emperor and assuming the name "Augustus" in 31 BCE. This ushered in the so-called "Golden Age of Rome," during which Roman civilization conquered the ancient world. It was also a good time for the Jews, as Caesar's edicts were reaffirmed. However, Augustus was succeeded by a series of awful and sometimes degenerate emperors, some of whose actions directly affected the Jews of Italy. For example, following the death of Augustus in 14 CE, the new emperor, Tiberius, exiled the Jews from Rome in 19 CE, probably for the transgression of proselytizing. Of the exiles, 4,000 young men of military age were shipped off to Sardinia, where they either fought brigands or worked in the salt mines in the southern part of the island. It is possible that these men were slaves of Jews who had been freed with informal manumissions and had become fully Jewish, but were not yet Roman citizens. Twelve years later, when the exile was rescinded after the death of Tiberius, not all of these 4,000 young men who survived returned to Rome. There are some very interesting theories about how many remained in Sardinia, introducing elements of Judaism into Sardinian culture through marrying local women. For example, Sardinia is the only part of the Roman Empire to use the name *Capo d'Anno* (Italian; *caput anni*, Latin) instead of the Roman name, September. The term is a direct translation of *Rosh ha-Shana*, the Jewish New Year. Sardinians also slaughter their animals with a sharp knife across their necks and hang the carcass so as to drain it of blood before roasting the animal, usually a lamb, on a spit over an open fire. Intriguing though these ideas are, there is no way of confirming this theory other than through distant oral memory.

A more verifiable event, recorded in the writings of the Jewish historian Josephus Flavius as well as in other primary sources, is the Jewish uprising in Judea in 66 CE during the reign of Vespasian, followed by the destruction of the Second Temple in the year 70 CE. After four years of fighting (67-79 CE), Rome re-took Jerusalem and burned the Temple, shipping thousands

Josephus Flavius (ca. 38-after 100 CE)

Born in Jerusalem to an aristocratic priestly family, Josephus was well-educated as well as well-connected. Upon the outbreak of the Jewish war against Rome in 66 CE he was appointed commander of the Galilee, but his forces lost to those of the Romans, who took him prisoner. When he appeared before Vespasian, the Roman commander, he foretold the commander's greatness, thus saving his own life. When Vespasian was proclaimed emperor, Josephus was freed, and he accompanied Titus, the emperor's son, on his siege of Jerusalem, serving as witness to the destruction.

Josephus moved to Rome, became a citizen, and was granted a pension. The Jews despised him and considered him a traitor.

His historical writing was probably done at the command of Vespasian. He wrote in Greek, the language of culture at that time. His volume *The War of the Jews* was sanctioned by the emperor, and, as such, was considered the truth. The fact that Josephus himself observed much of what he described, as well as his literary skill, makes this a powerful work.

He wrote other works, including *The Antiquities of the Jews*, which contain a number of Roman documents testifying to the Roman attitude toward diaspora Jewish communities. Most of these are in Book 14 of *The Antiquities*.

of Jewish war prisoners to Rome, where they were paraded in traditional Roman style down the main paved roads in front of throngs of Roman celebrators. This was later commemorated in the Arch of Titus with its magnificent details of this parade, including the depiction of the *Menorah* taken from the Temple. The only ones not celebrating were Rome's Jews, who quickly got to work raising money to redeem their co-religionists from slavery by "buying" them. It is interesting to note that the Roman Jewish community did not suffer from the rebellion in Judea, perhaps because the Romans saw so many Jews as Roman citizens as well as neighbors. Whatever the reason, it took great effort on the part of local Jews to raise enough money to redeem such a large number of people. The redemption led to a rapid rise in the population numbers of the Jews in the imperial capital. The Jews were required to continue paying the half shekel, but now this money, labeled *fiscus judaicus*, went into the imperial treasury. The tax was broadened to include all Jews, not just those who had been paying the half shekel to the Jerusalem Temple. It was collected until the fourth century, when it was abolished by the Emperor Julian (361-363 CE), but it became the prototype for special taxes on Jews in the Middle Ages.

According to tradition, a smaller group transported over to Rome was an upper class of Jews made up of four Judean families, which were probably not enslaved. These were the *Min ha-Tapuhim, Min ha-Adumim, Min ha-Zekeinim,* and *Min ha-Anavim* families, whose names were gradually translated into De'Pomi, De'Rossi, De'Vecchi and Piatelli or Anau. These aristocrats brought a sophisticated element to Italian Jews, which added to the mix of re-creation of community.

As the Jewish community expanded, naturally, more than one new *scuola* was founded to deal with these larger numbers. It also was natural for the Jews who came from Jerusalem and from Alexandria to set up their own centers. There were already differences in customs, and every group tenaciously held on to its own. Paper had not yet reached the west, and printing was not to be invented for centuries, so there were very few hand-written collections of manuscripts, yet each *scuola* had its own Torah scrolls. We can only guess whether they were locally produced or brought over from Israel. It is surmised that with the influx of Judeans came some professional scribes, but we do have information that points to a low level of study and lack of rabbinic leadership until that time.

After the destruction of the Second Temple, the Jews rebounded by focusing on religious law and spirituality centered on the academy and the synagogue. With the founding of the academy at Yavneh in 70 CE on the central coastal plain of Israel, the period of the Mishna/Talmud was inaugurated. This overlapped with the general historical period of Rome ruling Palestine and a revived Persian (Sassanid) Empire ruling the Babylonian center, and the Palestinian academies were rivaled by the academies in Babylon. Although there was only one Mishna, produced in Roman-controlled Palestine, there were two Talmuds, one from each major center.

The Mishna was the redaction of the oral law that had been passed down through the generations and traced back, according to tradition, to Moses. It was kept in oral form until the period of the Roman persecution of Jews in Palestine. At that time, fearful that the traditions would be lost as a result of the executions of so many sages, the remaining sages made the decision to write it down. The resulting six volumes that make up the Mishna, compiled by Judah Ha-Nasi, are in clear and concise Hebrew and divided by subject matter. But the development of oral tradition continued, and, again fearful of the loss of the tradition, a new generation of sages decided that the next step was to write down this next level of law—this time in the Aramaic that was the *lingua franca* of the Middle East, a result of the Babylonian conquest centuries earlier. This was compiled in two editions: the Palestinian version, called the *Talmud Yerushalmi*, was completed circa 400 CE, and the Iraqi version, called the *Talmud Bavli* (Babylonian Talmud), circa 500 CE. The focuses of the legal discussions of the two differ somewhat, with the former dealing more with laws connected to the land of Israel, and the latter with the realities of diaspora life. It was inevitable, therefore, that the Babylonian Talmud came to be studied wherever Jews re-created their communities.

The Palestine communities kept in touch with the Jews of the Roman Empire, centered in Rome itself, by collecting monies, known as *aurum coronarum*, for the upkeep of the center of Jewish intellectual life in Yavneh, which continued despite the destruction of the Temple, and by sending scholars to visit Rome.

One group of visitors, in 95 CE, included Rabban Gamliel II, head of the Academy, R. Joshua ben Hananya, R. Eleazar ben Azarya, and R. Akiva. The deputation came with the urgent task of securing the withdrawal of an edict against Judaism which was about to be issued by the emperor Domitian. The matter was so urgent that the sages traveled during the *Succot* holiday, and when they arrived in Rome they were hospitably hosted by a "philosopher," possibly Josephus the historian. The immediate danger that they feared was averted either by successful pleading or due to the fortuitous death of the Emperor.

While they were in Rome, it became clear to these visiting scholars that the level of knowledge among the populace was not very high. They took it upon themselves to help organize the community and deal with a new legal factor that had developed, namely that of converts to Judaism who were *metuentes*, or "half-way Jews" or "God-fearers." Despite the contempt for Judaism expressed by many Romans, such as Tacitus, there was a growing number of people who were attracted to monotheism and Jewish ceremonies and laws, in particular those connected with the Sabbath. In other words, the Jewish lifestyle itself was attractive. People of all classes appear in Talmudic sources as "half-way Jews," and many took the final step and became full Jews.

To improve the education of the community, the scholars helped set up a new *bet medrash* based on the idea of the *yeshiva* or academy, using the principles of teaching established in Palestine. The man who was sent from Yavneh to direct this was R. Matityahu ben Kharash. It should be noted that educating the larger Jewish populace was always a goal of the Jewish sages. Education was provided in part through legal guidance, but also through the activities of the preachers in the synagogues who, through public sermons, would communicate Jewish wisdom to all who attended, including the women and children. The sermon was a main tool of public education, and the literature used to illustrate various points included among other sources the *Midrash Aggada,* or homiletic commentaries, which date to the period of the Mishna. Another literary development of that period which was used as a means of education was the *piyyut* or liturgical poem, which was read during the prayer service.

In the middle of the second century, another visit was made, this time by R. Shimon bar Yohai and R Eleazar ben Yossi. They too came at a time of danger for the Jews of Palestine, and they too were received by the emperor. We have records in the Talmud of their impressions of Rome and of how they helped R. Matityahu ben Kharash with certain points of law. The effect of these visits was to cement the connection of the Jews of Italy to the Jews of Palestine, and to ensure that the customs they followed were those of the Palestine scholars. This laid the groundwork for what later developed, across the Alps in the Rhineland, into Ashkenazi Jewry. Middle Eastern Jews followed decisions made in Babylonia, which is present-day Iraq.

By this time the Jews in Rome had become acculturated in many ways. For example, many funerary artifacts found, especially the burial plaques, point to the use of a common workshop, as do the decorative motifs. Funerary inscriptions reflect naming practices, and demonstrate the use of Latin names. Yet as Romanized as they became, they also asserted their Jewish identity, and struggled to balance their Jewishness with the attractions of Roman culture. The plaques' epitaphs, for example, show that Jews proudly defined themselves in terms of what they did for the synagogue, and thus for the community.

Religious unrest grew throughout the Roman Empire in the second century. Because many cults practiced various forms of self-mutilation, Emperor Hadrian (r. 117-138 CE) categorically prohibited such acts, including the circumcision practiced by the Jews. This was one of the factors leading to the Bar Kokhba revolt in Palestine (132-135 CE), and the suppression of that revolt added many more Jews to the populations of

Rome and southern Italy. The next emperor revoked this law, but although circumcision was allowed for Jews, it was forbidden for others, namely to converts. A few years later, in 204 CE, the emperor Septimus Severus forbade conversions to either of the two monotheistic religions, Judaism and Christianity.

Christianity, born in the land of Israel, was known in Rome at an early stage. Both Peter and Paul, two of the most important shapers of the substance and form of the new religion, had travelled to the imperial city, and both were executed there by the emperor Nero. Christians were in

---

Roman Decrees from
The Antiquities of the Jews **by Josephus Flavius**
Book 14, Chapter 10.

... Now it does not please me that such decrees should be made against ... [the Jews] whereby they are forbidden to live according to their own customs, or to bring in contributions for common suppers and holy festivals, while they are not forbidden so to do even at Rome itself.... I permit these Jews to gather themselves together, according to the customs and laws of their forefathers, and to persist therein....

... [the Jews] could not go into their armies, because they are not allowed to bear arms, or to travel on the Sabbath days, and they must procure themselves those sorts of food which they have been used to eat from the times of their forefathers. I do therefore grant them a freedom from going into the army ... and permit them to use the customs of their forefathers in assembling together for sacred and religious purposes, as their law requires, and for collecting oblations necessary for sacrifices....

... I have at my tribunal set these Jews, who are citizens of Rome, and follow the Jewish religious rites ... from going into the army, on account of the superstition they are under....

... Those Jews that are our fellow citizens of Rome ... demonstrated that they had an assembly of their own, according to the laws of their forefathers, and this from the beginning, as also a place of their own, wherein they determined their suits and controversies with one another. Upon their petition therefore to me, that these might be lawful for them, I give order that these their privileges be preserved, and they be permitted to do accordingly.

...we have decreed, that as many men and women of the Jews as are willing so to do, may celebrate their Sabbaths, and perform their holy offices, according to the Jewish laws....

general suspect because they refused to follow the pagan Roman rituals. By the second century, Christianity was Judaism's main rival for converts. But Christians were persecuted more than Jews were at this point, for the Jews had the historical legal right to practice their religion openly. The Jews were even included in the edict of 212 CE, promulgated by the emperor Caracalla, which made all free inhabitants of the Empire into Roman citizens. However, the third century was one of bloody palace revolts and anarchy in the empire, with the Romans suffering from high taxes and external attacks, mainly from the north and the east. By this time there were Jewish settlements in Bari, Oria, Otranto, and Taranto in the south, as well as in the Sicilian cities of Syracuse, Palermo, Catania, and Messina.

The Edict of Milan of 313 CE gave religious freedom to all, thus sealing the fate of paganism. Emperor Constantine (r. 324-337) then took two steps with wide historical repercussions: he moved the Empire's capital from Rome to Byzantium, along the western side of the narrow straits separating Europe from Asia, and he sided with Christianity against all other religions, making it the official religion of the Empire. He renamed the city Constantinople, and under the influence of his mother Helena, a deeply religious convert to Christianity, passed the first of a long list of anti-Jewish laws. Whether or not he converted to Christianity himself is a matter of dispute, but the laws he instituted set the tone for what would become the Eastern Roman Empire, or Byzantium, after the split with Rome became formal in 395 CE.

One of the most important sources of information on Jewish life at the time of Imperial Rome is Roman law, much of which survived in collections like the Theodosian Codex (438 CE) and the Justinian Code (528 CE, revised 534 CE). Scholars can trace the laws passed by pagan Rome, as they were adopted by Christian Rome, as modified by Teutonic Rome. In other words, a law could be reshaped three times, or could stand unchanged no matter who was ruling. In a way it is astonishing to see how much attention was paid to the Jews, who were such a small portion of the population. But there was a kind of logic to the passage of these laws within the framework of Christian theology: if the Church was the true heir of the Roman Empire, then it had to honor the laws passed by the earlier rulers.

When an edict was issued by an emperor, it was published and distributed to the governors of the provinces, who promulgated it to the areas under their control. Its permanence, or continuity beyond the lifetime of the emperor, was stressed. With the growing identification of the Empire with Christianity, the words used to describe the Jews took on a tone of condemnation, with the strongest pejorative terms appearing in laws dealing with proselytes. One of them, passed by Constantine in 315 CE, reads:

> We wish to make it known to the Jews ... that if, after the enactment of this law, any one of them dares to attack with stones or some other manifestation of anger another who has fled their dangerous sect and attached himself to the worship of God, he must speedily be given to the flames and burnt together with all his accomplices. Moreover, if any one of the population should join their abominable sect and attend their meetings, he will bear with them the deserved penalties.

In other words, Jews were not allowed to punish anyone who left Judaism for Christianity ('the worship of God'), showing us first that there were converts from among the Jews, and second that the Jews physically punished them for leaving their religion.

Another item of note is that this law is written using pejorative language in connection with Judaism, in this case "dangerous sect" and "abominable sect." This language was to continue being used by later lawmakers and would make its way into the language of Church law as well. The punishment is possibly this severe because the lawmakers knew that only a strong threat of punishment would keep the Jews from acting against apostasy.

Who would have converted to Christianity at this time from among the Jews? Jews who were weak in their beliefs, Jews who were ambitious politically, and possibly also converts to Judaism who now found that Christianity provided monotheism without the burden of the commandments. Of course, there was also the theological appeal of Christianity, with its promise of salvation.

One of the three categories of laws concerning Jews regarded their relations with the government. As unwilling as the Christian emperors were to recognize the Jews as a "permitted religion," they had to preserve this direct continuity between the old and the new rule. Thus they focused on accepting Judaism as a religion rather than the Jews as a nation. They maintained the exemptions of Jews from duties that could lead to profaning the Sabbath, and they recognized the synagogue as the center of Jewish religious life, but in the political sphere, the status of the Jews moved from exemption to legal discrimination. This was often accomplished through the laws of the second category, which were those concerning the relationships between non-Jews and Jews. Only in the third category, laws concerning the relationships between Jews and other Jews, was very little changed.

Another anti-Jewish law, passed by Constantius in 339, reads:

> This pertains to women who live in our weaving factories and whom Jews, in their foulness, take in marriage. It is decreed that these women are to be restored to the weaving factories. This prohibition is to be preserved for the future lest the Jews induce Christian women to share their shameful lives. If they do this they will subject themselves to a sentence of death.

Without going into explanations about the weaving factories, which housed female slaves and were a source of income for the imperial household, or into why Jews would want to marry such women, we find here a prohibition against intermarriage. The slaves, according to the text, seem to have converted to Christianity, which appealed very much both to the oppressed and to women. There is a Christian religious objection to intermarriages, but there probably was an economic one as well, for Jews are obliged to free fellow Jews from slavery, and in this milieu Jews would not have married women without their being Jewish as well. If these women worked in the imperial weaving factories, they were probably very skilled and therefore desirable as laborers. The factory owners would have taken a loss seeing the women convert to Judaism and then be redeemed from the factory.

Another law passed by Constantius concerning the Jews read:

> If any one among the Jews has purchased a slave of another sect or nation, that slave shall at once be appropriated for the imperial treasury. If, indeed, he shall have circumcised the slave whom he has purchased, he will not only be fined for the damage done to that slave but he will also receive capital punishment. If, indeed, a Jew does not hesitate to purchase slaves—those who are members of the faith that is worthy of respect—then all the slaves who are found in his possession shall at once be removed. No delay shall be occasioned, but he is to be deprived of the possession of those men who are Christians.

By prohibiting Jews from owning slaves or trading in slaves, the emperor was not only trying to stop any conversion to Judaism, he was also attacking the economic life of the Jews, for this was a slave-based society. The Jews were now at a disadvantage in the economic marketplace.

A law further curbing the rights of Jews was passed by Theodosius II in 439 CE:

> No Jew ... shall obtain offices and dignities; to none shall the administration of city service be permitted; nor shall any one exercise the office of a defender of the city. Indeed, we believe it sinful that the enemies of the heavenly majesty and of the Roman laws should become the executors of our laws—the administration of which they have slyly obtained—and that they, fortified by the authority of the acquired rank, should have the power to judge or decide as they wish against Christians, yes, frequently even over bishops of our holy religion themselves, and thus, as it were, insult our faith.

The Jews were thus prohibited from holding public office, a position of honor that all citizens had previously been permitted. For Christians, who believed that Christianity was the heir to Judaism and that it supplanted the first monotheistic faith, it was a slap in the face to have Jews in positions of power over them. It did not matter that by this point in time holding a public office had become a financial burden to the holder. But that was not the end of this law, for Theodosius continued:

> ... We forbid that any synagogue shall rise as a new building. However, the propping up of old synagogues which are now threatened with imminent ruin is permitted....

This was not a new idea, but one that was revived from time to time. The Jews tended to react to it by setting up places of prayer in the private homes of wealthy members of the community. With the end of the Roman Empire, Jewish communities were shrinking anyway, and there was little need for large places of worship.

A last anti-Jewish law was passed by Emperor Justinian in 531 CE:

> Since many judges, in deciding cases, have addressed us in need of our decision, asking that they be informed what ought to be done with witnesses who are heretics, whether their testimony ought to be received or rejected, we therefore ordain that no heretic, nor

Glass products of Jewish artisans who brought glassmaking to Italy from
Israel. Aquileia—the northeastern outpost of the Roman Empire
(Photograph, R. Fodde collection, from the Aquileia Archaeological Museum)

even they who cherish the Jewish superstition, may offer testimony
against orthodox Christians who are engaged in litigation, whether
one or the other of the parties is an orthodox Christian.

Losing the right to bear witness in court against an orthodox Christian was
a final disability added on to the list of the other social, economic, civil,
political, and religious disabilities referred to above. But by the time this
last law was passed, the split of the Empire was formal (having occurred in
395 CE), and the attacks of over a century on Italy and Rome brought about
the end of the Roman Empire in the West. In a short time, the Eastern
Empire, also known as Byzantium, ended the Palestine academy system,
and the ties of Italian Jews to this religious center also came to an end.
Italy's Jews were now on their own.

Goths, Lombards, and Franks invaded Italy from the north, fusing,
over the next three centuries, into Italians. Only the churches provided
continuity, with the popes gaining political power and pitting groups
against each other until, in 754 CE, Pope Stephen II went to crown Pepin II
king in France. In return, the pope was given the rulership of central Italy,
which underscored his temporal rule. In the jousting over whether church
or state had more power, Charlemagne's arrival in Rome, and Pope Leo III's
success in crowning him Holy Roman Emperor in 800 CE, seemed to place
the papacy above the secular ruler.

Recommended Reading

Cappelletti, Silvia. *The Jewish Community of Rome from the Second Century BCE to the Third Century CE*. Leiden: Brill, 2006.

Leon, Harry J. *The Jews of Ancient Rome*. Peabody, MA: Hendrickson Publishers, 1995.

Linder, Amnon, ed. *The Jews in Roman Imperial Legislation*. Detroit: Wayne State University Press, 1987.

Rutgers, Leonard V. *The Jews in Late Ancient Rome: Evidence of Cultural Interaction in the Roman Diaspora*. Leiden: Brill, 2000.

Chapter 3

THE MEDIEVAL SOUTH

During the period of transition from the ancient world to the medieval one, people tended to leave cities throughout Italy, thereby avoiding both the invasions and the changes in regime that accompanied them. Many Italians moved into fortified villas, which were owned by wealthy landowners and protected by their small private militias. Individuals would seek this protection and enter into a relationship of personal dependency with the landowner.

The sixth century in particular brought death and destruction at the hands of the invading Germanic tribes, who brought with them into Italy ideas of Arianism—a variant of Christianity later labeled heretical

Timeline

GENERAL		JEWISH
Pope Gregory I (the Great)	590—601	
Arab rule over Sicily	827—1061	Pact of 'Umar applied to Jews and Christians
	913—c. 982	Shabtai Donnolo
	1017—c. 1060	Ahimaaz ben Paltiel
Norman invasion of Sicily and South Italy	1061	
First Crusade	1096	
	1160—1176	Benjamin of Tudela's travels
Pope Innocent III	1198—1216	
Fourth Lateran Council	1215	Anti Jewish laws
Sixth Crusade	1228	
Founding of University of Bologna	c. 1088	
	1261—1328	Immanuel of Rome
Dante	1264—1321	
House of Anjou rules South	1265	
Inquisition	1268	
Aragon rules South	End of thirteenth century	
	1288	Expulsion of Jews from Kingdom of Naples
Anti Jewish actions by Dominicans	1290	"Blood libel" against Jews of Aquila
	1306, 1322, 1394	Jews expelled from France
Popes in Avignon	1309—1378	
Black Death	1348—1351	
	1391	Attacks on Jews of Spain

by mainstream Christians—and paganism. But Roman Catholicism held firm, and during the early period of invasions, the local churches and the Papacy actively participated in providing aid to the poor. They claimed jurisdictional power over the rival Byzantine patriarchs in Constantinople, and their alliance with the Carolingians—the new dynasty north of the Alps—in the eighth century made it possible for a temporal papal state to come into being.

The popes became masters of "The Republic of Saint Peter," and this temporal power was established by Gregory the Great (590-604 CE), who was the key figure in determining its treatment of the Jews. His policies on Jews, both positive and negative, were spelled out in his various letters. Out of the over one hundred letters written by Gregory the Great, twenty-eight of them concern Jews. His generally positive attitude toward them was probably due to a combination of influences, such as his training as a jurist immersed in pure law, his perceptions of Jewish economic power, and his apocalyptic belief that the willing conversion of Jews to Christianity would usher in the Second Coming and the End of Days. In the power struggle with the Byzantine Church and sectarianism, he also planned to use the laws enforcing the proper relationship between Christians and Jews as a way to centralize papal authority. He protected

Gregory to Fantinus, Papal Administrator of Palermo, Sicily. October 598

A while ago, we wrote to Victor, our brother and fellow-bishop, that some Jews sent us a petition that synagogues situated in the city of Palermo had been unreasonably occupied by him. He should delay any consecration of them until the case be clarified whether this thing had actually been done, lest injury or prejudice should come to the case. And, indeed, we cannot believe that our aforesaid brother, having regard for his priestly office, could have done anything improper.

But we found from the report of Salerio, our notary, who was afterwards there, that there was no reasonable cause for taking possession of those [synagogues], and that they had been improperly and rashly consecrated. For this reason, we recommend that it be your decision that even though consecrated, they should be returned to the Jews. The sons of the illustrious patrician Venantio, and Urbico the Abbot, may estimate the value of the synagogues themselves with the guest-chambers that are under them or annexed to their walls, and the adjoining gardens....

Also, the manuscripts and ornaments that have been carried off be in like similarly returned.... ("Gregorius Magnus," *Patrologia Latina*, vol. 76, book 9, Letter 55.)

those rights which were theirs by law, overriding local bishops who had confiscated synagogues and forcibly converted Jews. Again and again he wrote that conversion had to be authentic. Upon discovering, for example, that Bishop Victor of Palermo in Sicily had confiscated a synagogue and had consecrated it to Christianity, Gregory ordered that proper compensation be paid and that all books and ornaments that had been seized be returned to the Jewish community. Roman law had only compensated Jews for their land; this new law expanded these protections to their books and ornaments as well. One letter's detailed description of the synagogue gives us clues as to what it looked like—a main building, with rooms or small buildings nearby used as inns, hospitals, and gardens, in a kind of compound. We see that they also had books, those rare and valuable objects that were at the time hand written on parchment or vellum, and probably included Bibles and Talmuds, as well as Hebrew poetry that would be read during prayers. Yet Gregory I wavered on the issue of Jews owning Christian slaves, and in the end decided against it, thereby diminishing the Jewish capability to compete in the economic world.

The south of Italy, to which many of these letters were addressed, soon came under the control of Byzantium, or the Eastern Roman Empire, for Constantinople constantly tried to expand its control. Jews were attracted to the commercial centers in the south, such as Oria, Bari and Otranto, and even more so the big cities of Sicily such as Palermo, Syracuse and Messina. Sicily, by contrast, was about to be invaded by a totally different army, that of the Arabs coming from North Africa, the third power trying to gain political and religious control of Italy.

Islam, born in Arabia in 622 CE, was the third monotheistic religion to come into existence. Ten years later, after Arabia was almost entirely converted to Islam, and the tribes were organized as one people to invade northward into the central part of the Middle East, the Prophet Muhammad died. The crisis of leadership was solved by the election on the part of the tribal leaders of deputies, or caliphs, to continue the plan of the spreading of Islam. The caliph held in his hands military, political, and religious leadership, just as Muhammad had. The first four elected caliphs led armies into the Middle East and started on the long road across North Africa, conquering relentlessly. After the fourth caliph, Ali, founder of Shi'i Islam, died, the first Arab kingdom was set up, headed by the Umayyad family, who relocated the capital from Mecca to Damascus. By the time the Umayyads were overthrown by the Abbasid dynasty in 750 CE, Arab armies had crossed from Morocco into Spain, and had reached central France before being defeated for the first time. On the eastern front, the armies had reached the borders of China and had even entered India. The Arabs then made plans for the northern Mediterranean.

Sicily was invaded in 827 CE by an army of the semi-autonomous Aghlabids, a breakaway dynasty centered in Tunisia. This dynasty was, in turn, overthrown by a Shi'i counter-caliphate, that of the Fatimids. This group would shortly move to Egypt and set up a new capital in Cairo, rivaling the Abbasid capital in Baghdad. Arab control over Sicily and its attacks on southern Italy lasted until 1061.

At the same time that there was a crisis in leadership upon the death of Muhammad, there was a minor crisis over the fact that most of the people in the direct route of the invasion were not pagans but monotheists. Pagans could be forcibly converted, but monotheists could not. The decision was enacted that any people with a written scripture that was monotheistic in its beliefs would have the choice of retaining its religion on condition that its members become second class citizens, known as "Protected People," or *Dhimmi* . A type of contract was drawn up, generally called the "Pact of 'Umar," which contained socially, religiously, and politically discriminatory clauses; economic discrimination was already enforced in the form of two taxes, one on land and the other a poll tax (*jizya*) levied on every able-bodied man of army age.

Thus, when the Arabs invaded Sicily, Jews were tolerated and protected as long as they behaved according to the prescribed rules. The influence of the Arab culture was strong on the Jews of Sicily and of southern Italy in general. While the Arabs were often not seen as the originators of cultural ideas, they readily imitated what they saw around them by absorbing aspects of the local culture, fusing it with other admired cultures they encountered, and adding their own aesthetic elements. They thus assimilated Greek philosophy and science, Byzantine and Persian art, Jewish and Christian theology, and Roman law and government. They brought to Sicily and southern Italy not only the desire to translate everything into Arabic, but also many intellectual and cultural ideas that they had acquired along the way, like the so-called Arabic numerals, the concept of zero, and algebra. It is said that they introduced the lemon, the orange, and the sugar cane, as well as dates, mulberry bushes, and cotton, into Italy, along with Middle

The Pact of 'Umar, Seventh Century

In the name of Allah, the Merciful, the Beneficent.

This letter is addressed to Allah's servant 'Umar, the Commander of the Faithful, by the Christians of such-and-such city. When you advanced against us, we asked you for a guarantee of protection for our persons, our offspring, our property, and the people of our community, and we undertook the following obligations toward you, namely:

We shall not build in our cities or in their neighborhood new monasteries, churches, convents, or monks' cells. We shall not repair, by night or by day, any of them that have fallen into ruin or which are situated in the Muslims' quarters.
We shall keep our gates wide open for passersby and travelers. We shall give three days' food and lodging to all Muslims who pass our way.
We shall not shelter any spy in our churches or in our dwellings, nor shall we hide him from the Muslims.
We shall not teach the Koran to our children.
We shall not hold public religious ceremonies. We shall not seek to convert anyone. We shall not prevent any of our kin from embracing Islam if they so desire.
We shall show respect to the Muslims and shall rise from our seats when they wish to sit down.
We shall not attempt to resemble the Muslims in any way with regard to their dress …. We shall not speak as they do….
We shall not ride on saddles.
We shall not gird swords nor bear weapons of any kind, or carry them with us.
We shall not engrave inscriptions on our seals in Arabic.
We shall not sell wines.
We shall clip the forelocks of our head.
We shall always dress ourselves in our traditional fashion….
We shall not display our crosses or our books anywhere in the Muslims' roads or in their marketplaces. We shall only beat our clappers in our churches very softly. We shall not raise our voices when reciting the service in our churches, nor when in the presence of Muslims. Neither shall we raise our voices in our funeral processions….
We shall not take any of the slaves that have been allotted to the Muslims.
We shall not build our homes higher than theirs.

We accept these conditions for ourselves and for the members of our sect, in return for which we are to be given a guarantee of security. Should we violate in any way these conditions which we have accepted and for which we stand security, then there shall be no covenant of protections for us, and we shall be liable to the penalties for rebelliousness and sedition…. (Al-Turtushi, *Siraj al-Muluk*, 229-30. [Arabic])

Eastern musical instruments. But most important of all they introduced technology for the manufacture of paper, which they had learned about from the Chinese.

Within the context of Arab rule in Sicily and constant conquests and reconquests of sections of southern Italy from Byzantium, the Jews in southern Italy flourished. After centuries for which we have very few primary sources originating from this area, the curtain lifts briefly, presenting us with some particularly significant documents.

Shabtai Donnolo (913-ca.982) was a Jewish physician and writer on medicine, living in Oria on the Adriatic coast. We can presume that he was not only knowledgeable in medical and pharmaceutical matters, but that he also had command of many languages, including Latin, Greek, Hebrew and colloquial Italian. He wrote the *Book of Remedies* (*Sefer ha-Mirkakhot*) in Hebrew, which was the first serious medical book known to be written since the fall of Rome. He also wrote a commentary on the *Sefer Yetzira* or *Book of Creation*, which was the earliest extant Hebrew text of systematic speculate thought. Probably written in Hebrew in Palestine during the period of the Mishna-Talmud, the *Book of Creation* deals with both cosmology and cosmogony, that is, with questions of creation and order in the world. Its obscure style and brevity—it is only 1600 words long, and divided into six *mishnayot*—allows for two types of interpretation: one philosophical and one mystical.

**Shabtai Donnolo
(913-982 CE)**

Born in Oria, southern Italy, Shabtai Donnolo was captured by Arab raiders when he was twelve. After being ransomed by relatives, he remained in southern Italy, studying medicine, pharmacology, and astronomy, as well as classical Jewish subjects, Hebrew, Greek, and Latin.

Writing in Hebrew, Donnolo composed *Sefer ha-Mirkahot (Book of Remedies)*, the first book of its kind in Europe, and probably the first serious medical book written in Italy after the fall of Rome. Interestingly, the book shows that Greek-derived medical knowledge had not yet been affected by Arab medical knowledge.

His book *Sefer Hakhmoni* is a commentary on the older *Sefer Yetzira*, and reflects his scientific and rational background in his attempts to remove anthropomorphic elements in the Bible that refer to God, as well as his scientific explanation of Creation.

Shabtai Donnolo reflects the high level of culture and knowledge of the Jewish communities of southern Italy during his era.

Shabtai Donnolo, the rationalist, took the philosophical path, and in his commentary he removed all anthropomorphisms from the Hebrew Bible using scientific knowledge.

Story of the Four Captives

... The commander of a fleet, whose name was Ibn Rumahis, left Cordova, having been sent by the Muslim king of Spain, 'Abd al-Rahman al-Nasir. This commander of a mighty fleet set out to capture the ships of Edom [the Christians] and the towns that were close to the coast. They sailed as far as the coast of the land of Israel and swung about to the Greek sea and its islands. And they encountered a ship carrying four great scholars, who were travelling from the city of Bari to a city called Sefastin. They were on their way to a Kallah convention. Ibn Rumahis captured the ship and took the scholars prisoner. One of them was R. Hushiel the father of Rabbenu Hananel; one was R. Moses, the father of R. Hanokh, who was taken prisoner with his wife and his son R. Hanokh, who was only a lad. The third was R. Shemariah B. R. Elhanan. As for the fourth, I do not know his name. The commander wanted to violate R. Moses' wife, for she was exceedingly beautiful. She cried out in Hebrew to her husband, R. Moses, and asked him whether or not those who drown in the sea will be included in the resurrection of the dead. He replied unto her: "The Lord said: I will bring them back from Bashan; I will bring them back from the depths of the sea." Having heard his reply, she cast herself into the sea and drowned.

[R. Shemaria was sold in Alexandria, and became the head of that academy. R Hushiel was sold in Ifriqiya and became the head of the academy of Qairawan. R. Moses and R. Hanokh were sold at Cordova where he was redeemed and became the head of the academy there.] (Abraham Ibn Daud, *Sefer ha-Qabbalah*, edited and translated by Gerson D. Cohen [Philadelphia: JPS, 1967], 46-47 [Hebrew].)

The importance of Donnolo is not just in the fact that he was a creative individual. He was also a man representing the high level of usage of the Hebrew language in southern Italy, as well as proof of the availability of a variety of manuscripts. He did not live in a vacuum, but rather reflected the existence of a knowledgeable community of Jews in Oria who served as his audience. This idea is reinforced by the story "The Four Captives," as related by the Spanish Jewish scholar Abraham Ibn Daud in his *Sefer ha-Qabbala*, or *Book of Tradition*. In chapter seven, the story appears: the commander of the fleet of the Muslim king of Spain, ca. 970 CE, captured a ship carrying four great scholars who were traveling from the city of Bari. The four, R. Hushiel, R. Moses, R. Hanokh, and R. Shmarya, were sold in Egypt, Ifriqiya, and Cordova. Each proceeded to set up an academy of higher Jewish learning. What is important for our study is that they all set out from Bari, which, we may therefore presume, not only had educated Jews but an academy of the highest quality.

Another small item of interest appears in this tale, namely that when the commander wanted to violate R. Moses' wife, "She cried out in Hebrew to her husband, R. Moses, and asked him whether or not those who drown in the sea will be included at the time of the resurrection of the dead. He replied unto her: 'The Lord said: I will bring them back from Bashan; I will bring them back from the depths of the sea.' Having heard his reply, she cast herself into the sea and drowned." Notice that the language she used was Hebrew, and that the question that she asked was a *halakhic* one. In other words, women were also educated in Jewish laws and the Jewish language, and we can presume that, in keeping with Jewish tradition, rabbinic families arranged marriages among themselves so that their daughters and wives were brought up in the milieu of Torah and learning.

A third Jewish source from this period is the "Josippon," the historical narrative written in Hebrew by an anonymous southern Italian author which described the period of the Second Temple. A close reading of the text reveals that the writer had access to a variety of

Josippon

Written in Hebrew in southern Italy in the tenth century, this historical narrative describes the period of the Second Temple. The anonymous author includes the history of ancient Italy, devotes much space to the wars of the Jews against Rome, and concludes with the fall of Masada in 73 CE.

Internal clues point to southern Italy as the origin of the author, at the time that it was part of Byzantium, and the official language was Greek. The author, however, could not read Greek, but only Latin, and his main sources were a Latin manuscript of Josephus' *Jewish Antiquities*, the Latin version of *The Jewish War*, and the Latin version of the Apocrypha. His other sources were medieval chronicles.

The author was both a gifted historian and an excellent writer. His Hebrew is in Biblical style. The book's popularity throughout the Middle Ages may be due to the mistaken notion that it was written by Josephus. It was translated into many languages, and is often quoted by Jewish scholars.

This is a significant Jewish historical source for the Jews of southern Italy.

**Ahimaatz ben Paltiel
(1017-c. 1060 CE)**

Born in Capua, in southern Italy, Ahimaaz was a chronicler and a poet. In 1054 he moved to Oria, a more important southern Italian city which was the original base of his family. There he wrote *Megillat Ahimaaz*, a chronicle of his family geneology dating from the ninth century. In rhymed prose, this scroll describes a family that was prominent in leading communities in Italy as well as North Africa. It is therefore a significant Jewish historical source, despite some inaccuracies.

manuscripts, and, again, that Hebrew knowledge and creativity in Hebrew was alive and well in this part of Italy.

A fourth Jewish source is that of Ahimaatz ben Paltiel (b. 1017), who moved to Oria from Capua and wrote *Megilat Ahimaatz*, describing his genealogy in rhymed Hebrew prose. In addition to the historical data of his family, the scroll contains legends and fantastic tales, perhaps reflecting some of the popular literature arriving from the Middle East such as the tales in *A Thousand and One Nights*.

Sicily and southern Italy were soon to be invaded by a new force. In an attempt to gain power over the temporal rulers, the Papacy encouraged Normans to invade, and they did so in 1061. The Normans became the Pope's representatives in the newly

Innocent III

Concerning interest taken by Jews [Canon 67]

The more the Christians are restrained from the exaction of interest, the more does the treachery of the Jews in this matter increase, so that in a short time they exhaust the wealth of Christians. Wishing, therefore, to protect the Christians from this matter lest they be burdened excessively by the Jews, we ordain through synodal decree that if in the future they extort heavy and immoderate interest, no matter what the pretext be, Christians shall be withdrawn from association with them until the Jews give adequate satisfaction for their unmitigated oppression. Also the Christians shall be compelled, if necessary, through Church punishment from which an appeal will be disregarded, to abstain from business relations with the Jews.

We command the princes that they should not be hostile to the Christians because of this, but should rather seek to restrain the Jews from practicing such excesses.

And under threat of the same penalty we decree that Jews should be compelled to make good the tithes and dues owed to the churches which the churches have been accustomed to receive from the houses and other possessions of the Christians before they came into the possession of the Jews, regardless of the circumstances, so that the Church be safeguarded against loss.

That Jews should be distinguished from Christians in dress [Canon 68]

In some provinces a difference in dress distinguishes the Jews or Saracens from the Christians, but in certain others such a confusion has grown up that they cannot be distinguished by any difference. Thus it happens at times that through error Christians have relations with the women of Jews or Saracens, and Jews or Saracens with Christian women. Therefore, that they may not, under pretext of error of this sort, excuse themselves in the future for the excesses of such prohibited intercourse, we decree that such Jews and Saracens of both sexes in every Christian province and at all times shall be marked off in the eyes of the public from other peoples through the character of their dress.....

That Jews not be appointed to public offices [Canon 69]

Since it would be altogether too absurd that a blasphemer of Christ should exercise authority over Christians, we renew what the Toledo Council has wisely decreed in this matter. We forbid that Jews be preferred for public offices since in such capacity they manifest as much hostility to Christians as possible. If, moreover, any one should thus turn over an office to them, after due warning he shall be restrained by a severe punishment, as is fit, by the provincial council which we command to meet every year. Indeed, the association of Christians with such a Jewish official in commercial and other matters shall not be allowed until whatever he has gotten from Christians through the office is transferred to the use of poor Christians.... And he shall be dismissed in disgrace from the office which he has impiously assumed....

That Converts must not observe old Jewish customs [Canon 70]

Some converted Jews ... who came voluntarily to the waters of Holy Baptism, have not altogether cast off the old man in order to put on the new man more perfectly. Since they retain remnants of their earlier rites they confound the majesty of the Christian religion through such a mixture ... we therefore ordain that such persons must be restrained in every way by the prelates of the churches from the observance of their former rites. For in the observance of Christianity it is necessary that a healthy compulsion should preserve these Jews whom free will has carried to the Christian religion. It is a lesser evil not to know the way of the Lord than to retrace one's steps, after it has been acknowledged. ([Latin] Fourth Lateran Council, 1215, *Canons on Jews*, Fordham University website.)

formed Kingdom of Naples. The south became an intellectual crossroads, especially after the German Hohenstaufens married into the ruling Norman family; it also was the center of efficient government and tolerance. It was during Norman rule of the south that the Papacy reformed itself, not only attempting to rid the entire church of corruption but firmly setting in place the hierarchy of appointments, and the election of the pope by the cardinals.

The most notable pope of this period was Innocent III (1198-1216), and his attitude to the Jews is manifested in a variety of papal edicts.

Papal edicts are one primary source indicating the treatment of Jews during this period of time. Additionally, documents including tax records, communal records, and responsa survive. This last is a genre of Jewish law dating back to the post-Talmudic period (after 500 CE), when the dispersed Jewish communities directed difficult legal questions to the academies in Palestine or Iraq. The genre is of great significance, for the responses of the heads of the academies reflected not only Jewish law but Jewish life.

An unusual primary source that seems to come out of nowhere is a record of the travels of a Spanish Jew from Tudela named Benjamin. He recorded his voyages, which took place from 1160 through 1173 and ultimately took him to the Holy Land and the land of the academies, namely *Bavel* or Iraq. On his trip to the Holy Land, Benjamin traveled through northern Italy, specifically Genoa, Lucca, and Pisa, before visiting Rome. There are not that many sources discussing the Jewish communities of northern Italy during the period of the high middle ages other than those about Rome itself. We know that Lucca was important because it was on the overland route to and from France. It was the home birthplace of Moses ben Kalonymus, who moved to the Rhineland,

---

Benjamin of Tudela (second half of twelfth century CE)

The greatest medieval Jewish traveler, Benjamin left Tudela in northern Spain in either 1159 or 1167, returning in 1172. Recording his impression in his *Sefer ha-Massa'ot (Book of Travels)*, the author left one of the best primary sources of his time. He traveled through northern Spain and Provence before sailing to Genoa, from which he traveled to Pisa and Rome. His description of the Roman Jewish community is remarkable in its details. From there he headed south, describing Salerno, Amalfi, Brinidisi, and Otranto, all major Jewish settlements at the time, before heading east to Greece, Byzantium, and the Crusader-controlled Eretz Israel. The next leg of his journey took him through Syria and Iraq, around Arabia to Egypt, from there to Sicily, and finally home.

Benjamin of Tudela's account of the Mediterranean world, in this case Italy, is concise and objective. The Jewish communities he visited, the numbers of Jews, local economics, and local Jewish scholarship all interested him, but so did the non-Jewish world. His work is studied by medievalists of all areas, and has been translated in many other languages.

bringing Talmudic learning, mysticism, and religious poetry with him. Pavia comes up in the documents, as does Verona. But we can only guess at the details of Jewish life in these locales at the time that northern Italy began to grow in wealth and importance in part as a result of the Crusades.

The Crusades is a complicated subject that is often simplified into a desire on the part of Christian Europe to take the Holy Land from the Muslims, thereby making it safe for Christian pilgrims to visit their holy sites. However, there were also strong economic and political dimensions to the Crusades. Beginning in 1096 and ending with the sixth crusade, which was launched in 1228, Christian Europe did carve out some Crusader kingdoms in the eastern Mediterranean that lasted for a couple of hundred years. From the perspective of Italy, the physical movement of soldiers injected huge amounts of money into the economies of port cities in particular, as the city-states of Genoa, Pisa, and Venice supplied the soldiers coming from England, Germany and France with goods, food, and transportation. But few Italians served in the crusading armies. On their return trips, the Italian ships brought back Middle Eastern products to be sold in Italy, often for great profits.

This was the world visited by Benjamin of Tudela. He listed 200 Jewish families in Rome, which makes for a Jewish population of about 1,000 people. Going south from there to Naples, he describes a community numbering about 500 living on a "Jewish Street." Salerno had an even larger number of Jews, namely 1,500 in its Jewish quarter or *judaica*. Then he crossed the "boot," visiting Trani, Apulia, Taranto, Otranto and Brindisi before crossing the Adriatic to Greece. On his return trip, Benjamin visited Sicily, in which the Jews seem to have been well off under the Normans, and Palermo, which is described as having 1,500 Jews.

The communities of Jews Benjamin describes included people in all strata of society. International merchants were the most prominent members, and there were some physicians, but the majority of the people seem to have been involved in handicrafts. Other sources indicate that the three leading fields were the manufacturing of silk and the weaving and dyeing of fabrics. Two colors of dye specifically connected with Jewish craftsmen were red from henna and blue from indigo. The plants used for the dyes were often imported, and the secrets of the dye-making passed from one generation to the next. The Jewish dyers and weavers were so important that in Sicily King Frederick even made them into state monopolies for a while, beginning in 1231.

With the general synthesis of cultures which resulted in part from the Crusades, there eventually came a revival in learning which manifested itself in part in the establishment of universities. When students began to come to Bologna to attend lectures given by a group of legal experts who analyzed and adapted Roman law to the needs of medieval cities and guilds, thus formulating the notion of "common law," in contrast to royal or guild or town law), these students formed associations which led to the creation of a university with a specific curriculum. The model of Bologna was followed by Vicenza, Padua, Naples, Piacenza, Rome, Perugia, Pisa, Florence, Siena, and Pavia. The students first studied an arts curriculum, the "trivium" of grammar, rhetoric and logic, and then moved on to the "quadrivium" of arithmetic, geometry, astronomy, and music. Finally the student chose one of the higher curricula, namely law, theology, or medicine. Scholars agree that Jews lived in each of the university towns, but differ on whether or not Jews were allowed to attend the universities, let alone teach in them. The only definite information we have is that King Frederick brought Jacob Anatoli from Marseille to Naples, where the king set up a university in 1224. The brilliant king was interested in translating everything that he could, and Jacob Anatoli was a leading expert of translation, successfully translating the Arabic of the philosopher Averroes as well as a variety of Arabic astronomical works into Hebrew. These translations were one of the elements contributing to what came to be called the Renaissance. The Jews thus had a share in reconstituting the Aristotelian texts that were so vital for the new intellectual stage.

After King Frederick's death, his son Manfred took over his Italian holdings. He too was interested in translations from Arabic and Hebrew, and had his father's wide intellectual interests, but he was overthrown by Charles of Anjou, with the pope's backing, in 1265. During the following two decades, southern Italy was a fief of the pope until it passed to Aragon at the end of the thirteenth century. It was under the House of Anjou and the rule of Aragon that the situation of the Jews changed. This was when the edicts passed earlier by Pope Innocent III were fully enforced.

Under Innocent III (1198-1216), the Papacy had reached the height of its political and religious power. Like his papal predecessors, Innocent III was ready to continue the special privileges that the Jews had been granted by earlier church authorities. But that was all. He sought to enforce and expand older decrees, as we can see in the decrees passed by the Fourth Lateran Council, an international conference of theological experts that assembled to discuss Church doctrine in November 1215 in the Lateran church in Rome.

The first topic addressed was that of interest charged by Jewish lenders:

> ... We ordain ... that if they hereafter extort heavy and unrestrained interest ... Christians shall be withdrawn from association with them.... Also the Christians shall be compelled, if necessary, through Church punishment from which an appeal will be disregarded, to abstain from business relations with the Jews.

The Pope made it clear that the Christian princes who encouraged the Jews to money-lend, for this was lucrative for them, should cease doing so. The Jews, too, had to pay the tithes owed to the churches by Christians who had forfeited their property to the Jews.

What we see here is one of the first references to what was going to become a profession of great importance to the Jews—that of money-lending. This was usually a small business, and most borrowers were the peasants, craftspeople, and townspeople with small amounts of property; the princes and dukes were in a minority. The need for instant money that drove the populace to borrow could range from a bad harvest, a need to pay a provider of raw goods immediately, or the wedding of a child. To obtain the loan, the borrower had to give a surety, which could have been a cloak, a small piece of jewelry, or the title to a house. The interest on the loan, according to the Lateran Council edict, could not be exorbitant, but it did not specify how much was allowed. How many Jews were involved in money lending in the twelfth century is unknown, but it could not have been too many, as most Jews were still involved in crafts and trade. Notice too that the church made sure that if the property of a Christian was taken over by a Jew for non-payment, the Jew had to pay the tithe to the church instead of the Christian owner, ensuring that they had no loss and that the Jew had less gain.

The second topic addressed would lead to social isolation:

> In some provinces, a difference in dress distinguishes the Jews or Saracens from the Christians, but in certain others such a confusion

has grown up that they cannot be distinguished by any difference. This it happens at times that through error Christians have relations with the women of Jews or Saracens, and Jews or Saracens with Christian women. Therefore, that they may not, under pretext of error of this sort, excuse themselves in the future for the excesses of such prohibited intercourse, we decree that such Jews and Saracens of both sexes in every Christian province and at all times shall be marked off in the eyes of the public from other peoples through the character of their dress....

Segregation of Jews from Christians in all aspects of life can be traced to this edict, but the edict also raises some questions about sexual relationships. Did this law mean that there were Jewish and Muslim ("Saracen") prostitutes that Christians were visiting? Did it mean that there was intermarriage? Logic seems to point toward its being more likely that these were Christian prostitutes that non-Christians were visiting, as within the worlds of Jews and Muslims, women involved in prostitution would have been punished by their own families. Christian women answered instead to church law.

The third topic concerning Jews was the restatement of the rule that Jews could not hold public office, for this would give them power over true believers. Innocent III strengthened this by decreeing that Christians who would give offices to Jews would be punished. "Indeed, the association of Christians with such a Jewish official in commercial and other matters shall not be allowed until whatever he has gotten from Christians through the office is transferred to the use of poor Christians...." Boycotts of this nature were very powerful. Why would Jews have been placed in public offices in the first place? Some possible reasons are because they were more educated in things like accounting and drawing up laws, or because, as God-fearing men, they were perceived as trustworthy, or because their loyalty to the local ruler was absolute.

The fourth decree stated clearly that converts from Judaism to Christianity were not to observe any of the old customs of the Jews. This provides evidence that there were numbers of Jews who converted to Christianity, out of either belief or convenience.

The fifth was directly connected to the Crusades:

We command that the Jews ... shall be compelled by the secular power to remit interest on loans made to those setting out on

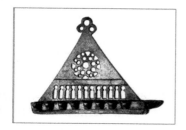

Chanukiyya (Hanukka oil lamp), brass, fourteenth century
(R. Fodde collection and photograph)

a Crusade; and until they remit it all faithful Christians shall …
refrain from every species of intercourse with them. For those,
moreover, who are unable at present to pay their debts to the Jews,
the secular princes shall provide by a useful delay, so that after they
begin their journey they shall suffer no inconvenience from interest,
until their death or return is known with certainty…

Crusaders without means, this decree stated, need not pay the
principal on their debts to their Jewish creditors until they returned. This
was a moratorium.

Based on these, we see that at the same time as various city-states
in Italy were expanding economically and intellectually, the papacy was
moving in the direction of confining the activities of the Jews.

The Fourth Lateran Council did not limit itself to these edicts;
it also recognized new orders that came into existence in an attempt to
combat Christian heresy. Unlike the first monastic order, that of the
Benedictines, which was founded in the sixth century and geared toward
praying, working, and obeying religious rules—and which contributed to
knowledge by copying manuscripts inside the walls of the "scriptorium"—
the new orders were not confined to monasteries. The Dominicans, called
the "Dogs of the Lord," hunted down heresy wherever it was suspected
of existing. The Franciscans were opposed to the sumptuousness of the
church and took vows of poverty; the members of the order wandered
around Europe begging and preaching. They were joined by another group,
the Flaggelants, which was a lay movement directed towards penance. By
1268, the Dominicans introduced the Inquisition to defend the Christian
world against heresy. It was only a matter of time before these groups would
directly affect the Jews.

One could say that attacks against Jews began in 1290 with the first
appearance of the "blood libel"—the scurrilous accusation that Jews use the

blood of Christians in Jewish rituals. The libel was directed by a Dominican friar at the Jews of Apulia in the south. The reaction of the Christian population was immediate and violent, and it began to spread. This was the beginning of the end of the Jewish communities in the south of Italy, for an order of expulsion from the Kingdom of Naples was made in 1288, and between 1290 and 1293 the Jewish communities were almost entirely destroyed. Many Jews converted to Christianity at around this time: it is recorded that 1,300 heads of families did so, and received tax remission as a result.

Recommended Reading

Ben-Sasson, H. H. "The Middle Ages." In *A History of the Jewish People*, edited by H. H. Ben-Sasson. London: Weidenfeld & Nicolson, 1976. 385-726

Mancuso, Piergabriele. *Shabbatai Donnolo's Sefer Hakhmoni.* Leiden: Brill, 2010.

Marcus, Jacob R. *The Jews in the Medieval World: A Source Book, 315-1791.* New York: Atheneum, 1969.

Roth, Cecil. *The History of the Jews of Italy.* Philadelphia: JPS, 1946.

Stow, Kenneth R. *Alienated Minority: The Jews of Medieval Latin Europe.* Cambridge, MA: Harvard University Press, 1992.

Chapter 4

The Move North

Usually, the historian has to guess about the specific details of the re-creation of a Jewish community. However, one major exception to this rule is the move of the Jews to the northern parts of Italy starting in the thirteenth century. By the fifteenth century, Jews were allowed to move to the Duchy of Urbino, which was first under the House of Montefeltro and then under the House of Della Rovere; to the Duchy of Ferrara (including Modena and Reggio), which was under the Este family; to the Duchy of Tuscany (including Florence and extending later to Siena and Pisa), which was under the Medici family; to the Duchy of Milan (including Cremona, Lodi, and Alessandria), under the Sforza dukes; to Piedmont under the House of Savoy; and to Mantua under the House of Gonzaga. Rome remained the center of Jewish life, and Papal control gradually extended to Ancona and Bologna and the Duchy of Urbino. The Republic of Venice was the last to allow the beginning of Jewish settlement. The Republic of Genoa continued to refuse to allow Jews to settle.

Timeline

GENERAL		JEWISH
Renaissance in north	c. 14th—16th centuries	
Direct Spanish control over Sicily	1412	
Pope Martin V	1414	
	1419	"Bull of benevolence"
Gutenberg dies	1468	First printed book in Hebrew
Ottoman Turks conquer Constantinople	1453	
Bernardino da Feltre	1475	Trent Blood Libel
	c. 1420—c. 1498	Judah Messer Leon
Unification of Spain	1492	Spanish Jewish expulsion, including Sicily
	1516	Ghetto Nuovo in Venice
	1470—1550	Ovadiah Sforno
	c. 1460s—1534	Gershom Soncino
	1553	Burning of Talmud in Rome
Cum Nimis Absurdum	1555	

Chapter 4. The Move North

Why was it that the Jewish population was able to settle so smoothly in most of northern Italy? Political rivalry between states and principalities had expanded into economic competition as well. Alliances were made and broken, and violence could erupt at any time. It was precisely this political fragmentation that favored Jewish settlement. Additionally, the political rivalry between these small states and principalities living so close to each other instigated cultural rivalry. The heads of the political entities were often still involved in the commercial operations that had led to their rise to power, and their lifestyle was not that of the aloof and remote imperial ruler but that of a wealthier member of the upper stratum of the city. They welcomed talent, even if it came from non-Christians, and so the Jews were able to share in Italian life. Gradually, the wealthy Jews began to behave like the heads of their small states, and became patrons of Jewish cultural life.

Finally, with the expansion of the economy in the north, in part due to the Crusades, there was a need for money. Large amounts of money were within the domain of Christian merchants and nobles, but smaller amounts could be found among the wealthier Jews living in the south of Italy, who were gradually being pushed out of international trade and the expanding commercial activity, for the medieval city and its guilds of merchants were Christian associations and monopolistic. Towns in the north sent representatives to these Jews, inviting them to resettle up north and open "loan banks," for consumer loans were forbidden by the Church—they were considered usury. The invitation was made to an individual, and the town drew up a contract, which regulated all of the details of this "loan bank" and the terms of settlement for the individual Jewish man. The loan-banker would either lend a large amount of money at once to the town or determine how much would be lent over the course of a year; the rate of interest would be set and a register would be kept. Money was an expensive commodity, so an interest rate of 25% was not unusual, and was lower than the rate charged by Christians. However, the Jewish man would want more than permission to buy or rent a house in the town. He would inform the town leaders that he was a married man, and had to move his family north as well. His family could have included a number of small children, and this would make it necessary to also bring at least one tutor. The family could have married children, and so the necessity to include sons-in-law or daughters-in-law arose. There could also be aging parents or in-laws to be considered. As practicing Jews, the loan banker and his family would also need a ritual slaughterer. In other words, the loan-banker's move up north meant the establishment of a nucleus for a new community, which was supplemented by Jewish merchants who would travel there with goods, and was eventually further supplemented by Jews from the south fleeing the persecutions taking place in that part of Italy.

The contract regulating the arrival and settlement of the loan-banker was called a *condotta* (conduct), and was fixed for a specific period. Its regulations detailed the loan banker's contract for the town leaders' loan, including the interest rate, what constituted pawns, and the conditions under which pawns could be sold. He could make other loans to local people as need arose. Transactions were generally on a small scale, and the Jewish loan-bankers became expert evaluators. The rates of interest were generally between 15% and 25%. What varied greatly were the personal rights of the Jewish loan banker. The *condotta* holder could transfer it to someone else or leave it to a son as an inheritance.

These small communities expanded as a result of the arrival of small groups of Yiddish-speaking Jews from Germany, who, fleeing the Black Death of 1348, settled in the area of Venice. Additionally, as a result of the expulsion of Jews from parts of France in 1394, a number of French Jews arrived in northern Italy, settling mainly in Savoy and Piedmont. They were labeled *Tedeschi* and *Provençali* by the local Italian Jews, and kept their separate customs for centuries before being absorbed by the larger group. The only remaining indication of the Jews who came from Provence and France and settled in Piedmont is the prayer ritual of APAM (Asti, Fossano, Moncalvo) kept alive in manuscripts handed down from father to son. A century later, the Jews coming from the southern part of Italy also retained their identities, in part by naming their synagogues after their towns of origin, if they arrived in large enough numbers.

The early Renaissance witnessed, among other things, a focus on Humanism with its revival of classical letters, its focus on individualism, its critical spirit, and its emphasis on secular concerns. But alongside this strand ran an undercurrent of sincere Christian religiosity and piety. The Popes were officially anti-Jewish and interested in upholding the anti-Jewish edicts of earlier times, yet in reality they often protected the Jews. The upper classes tended to be friendly, and they socialized to an extent with Jews of similar economic and intellectual interests. The middle class, fearing economic competition, tended to be more anti-Jewish, and the lower class bent whichever way the wind was blowing.

The Franciscan Observantine friars moved among the poor and heard their complaints about loans from Jews, which led them to become fanatical in their insistence on segregating Jews, on making them wear a badge, on forbidding them to employ Christians, and on forbidding usury. Three outstandingly fanatical itinerant preachers were Bernardino of Siena (d. 1494), his disciple John da Capistrano (1386-1456), and Bernardino da Feltre, considered by many to be the fomenter of the Trent Blood Libel of 1475. They traveled the length and breadth of Italy preaching against heresies and against the Jews, whom they saw as economic exploiters of the poor as well as non-believers. John da Capistrano added to the Franciscan anti-Jewish venom with his talent as a legal scholar and his inquisitorial powers, which allowed him access to ruling courts. He influenced, in particular, the situation of the Jews in Sicily and the Kingdom of Naples, who appealed to the various ruling popes for protection. The political fragmentation of northern Italy enabled harassed Jews to cross a nearby border to safely wait out an outburst of bigotry and then return, or remain in their new home and replant their community yet again.

In 1414 the schism within the church, a politically and religiously complex topic which focused on whether the pope had to be in Rome or could reside in Avignon, ended, and Pope Martin V was elected. The Jews set up a Vigilance Committee to send a delegation to the Holy See to ask for the Pope's protection and to confirm their historic rights. In 1419 the Pope's response took the form of a "bull of benevolence," which did just as was requested, adding that forced baptism of children was forbidden and that Jewish doctors could practice medicine as they wished.

In an attempt to prevent attacks provoked by envy, as well as to address the issue of a rivalry of conspicuous consumption among the Jews themselves, the Jews passed a series of sumptuary laws setting limits on types of clothing worn publicly, as well as on numbers of rings and brooches. The Jews also tried to unify the communities in their contributions for the expenses and gifts that the visits to the pope demanded. A decade later, the topic of the danger of the preaching friars was raised to the pope, and a new bull was issued forbidding them to preach against Jews and infringe on Jewish rights (1429). The next pope, Eugenius IV (1431), however, passed an anti-Jewish bull, and it wasn't until large sums of money had

Forli Sumptuary Laws, May 18 1418

... And in order to humble our hearts, and to walk modestly before our God, and not to show off to the Gentiles, we have agreed that from today, until the termination of the time already mentioned [1426], no Jew, male or female, of the above recorded Jewish communities, towns, or villages shall arrogantly wear a fur-lined jacket, unless of course it is black. Also the sleeves may not be open, nor be lined with silk, for that would be insolent. These existing fur-lined jackets, however, other than black, may still be worn, provided that the sleeves and the garments themselves are closed at the sides and at the back....

And no man should wear more than one gold ring which he may wear on any finger. Women should not wear more than two or three rings at a time.... (*Takanot Kadmoniyot*, ed. S.J. Halberstam [Breslau: 1887], 58-59.)

been paid that this bull was rescinded. This cost fell mainly on the Jews of Rome, as there was no real unified Jewish organization at that time.

A creative way of dealing with the problems of usury was the founding of the Monti di Pieta, public institutions that would lend money to the poor without interest. Theoretically this was a wonderful idea, but for it to succeed there had to be an initial large sum of money, a competent staff qualified to value the pledges and keep the accounts, and some way of paying for expenses. Many of these were started in the north using funds confiscated from Jewish loan bankers who were expelled from the local city. Some succeeded, but most did not. The Jews, in the meantime, merely moved to smaller cities where they set up new loan banks to which borrowers had to travel after the Monti failed. In the end, the expulsions spread Jewish settlement, rather than diminishing it. Two exceptional cases concerning the Monti di Pieta were Venice, in which the Jews' banks were in effect a second Monti, and Florence, where the Monti were government institutions.

The worst instance of anti-Jewish activity at this time took place in Trent, near the Austrian border. Bernardino da Feltre made a blood libel accusation against the Jews after the disappearance of a boy named Simon. His oratory so stirred up the populace that they attacked the Jews of Trent, killing some of them. This was also the first time that printing was used against the Jews, and broadsides appeared all over depicting the dead boy in gruesome detail. All of this so horrified the ruling dukes and princes that they finally set about protecting their Jews and tried to suppress the preachers. As a result of their actions, the Jews lived relatively peaceful lives for about a half-century.

While the Jews of northern Italy were undergoing trials and tribulations at the hands of the wandering preachers and fickle popes, the Jews of Spain were undergoing the horrors of the Inquisition and the expulsion of 1492. Small groups of Sephardic Jews had been arriving in Italy since the Reconquista began. Some of them settled in Sardinia, which was then Spanish possession, and others moved to the south of Italy. Larger groups came only after 1492, when tens of thousands of Jews were expelled. Most went to Portugal, Morocco, and the Ottoman Empire. Wherever they arrived in large enough numbers, these well educated, wealthy, and sophisticated Sephardim set up their own community structures, often taking over the local Jewish *kehilla* and imposing their own customs. Italy was one of the few places in which the local Jews had equal wealth and education to the new arrivals and refused to let them take over. The *scuola* in Rome, pitting Italians against Sephardim in a power struggle, a topic still debated by scholars, resulted in the appointment of Daniel da Pisa, a respected member of a famous Tuscan Jewish family, to act as conciliator. His well-crafted constitution provided for sixty men to administer the community, one-third from the upper class, one-third from the middle class, and the last third from the tax-paying poor.

Life also began to change for the Jews of Sicily, as the Spanish Catalan and Aragonese dynasties moved to include Sicily in the political sphere of Iberia. After withstanding for over a century attempts to place Iberian viceroys in charge of the island, in 1412 Sicily came under direct control of the Spanish dynasty. Therefore, when the Spanish edict of expulsion was promulgated in 1492, it included the Jews of Sicily.

The viceroy appealed to Sicilian Jews to convert in exchange for protection, just as Jews had been protected by the Crown from the beginning of the Middle Ages. The decision to convert or not was a personal one. How many Jews converted is in dispute, as is the actual number of Sicilian Jews there were to start with. Presuming that there were about 30,000-40,000 in 1492, perhaps half converted, and the rest left Sicily, mainly for the Kingdom of Naples. But there was a bout of the plague in Naples in 1493, followed by a French invasion the following year. This combination of factors spurred many more Jews not only to convert, but to return to Sicily, where they attempted to regain their property.

Ironically, the converts, described as *neofiti* in Sicily, were always seen as a separate group. Even though they were Christian, they had to pay special taxes, and there was no social acceptance of them, let alone intermarriage. But they were protected for a few years, until the Spanish Inquisition replaced the older, less virulent, local Inquisition in 1500. This was done in part for political reasons, for it strengthened the Spanish central government at the expense of the local powers. The actions of the Inquisition, however, were more restrained here than they were in Spain and only a couple of hundred *neofiti* were burned in the *auto-da-fés* by 1513. The *neofiti* were accused of Judaizing either passively, through adherence to old habits like not eating pork, or actively, for example by lighting Sabbath lights or by rejecting certain aspects of Christianity such as the Eucharist. They were also tracked down through their family ties and marriage patterns. Gradually, unless they left Sicily, these *neofiti*, who were mainly craftspeople, merged with the larger population. Some of the Jews in the Kingdom of Naples also converted, gradually merging with the Christians. Other Jews moved east to the Ottoman Empire or northward to the thriving city-states of Renaissance Italy.

Sephardic Jews also made their appearance in Venice, the last large city of northern Italy to allow Jews to settle. For centuries the Venetian Republic had only allowed Jews to visit the city for short intervals, mainly in order to trade. A small community grew in Mestre, and the Jews had to use boats of all sorts to reach Venice. It was not until the attacks of the French and Germans on the mainland, causing the Jews to come in as refugees, that the city masters finally allowed them to settle on one of the islands. They were allowed to remain behind the iron foundry, or *ghetto*. The *Ghetto Nuovo*, a walled in area, was built in 1516. Its gates were locked at night, thereby segregating and "protecting" the Jews. *Levantini* or Jews of Ottoman origin (in other words, Middle Eastern and Sephardic Jews), escaped the original segregation, but soon were forced to live in the enclosed area too, in the space known as the *Ghetto Vecchio*. Each community set up its own *scuola*, following its own rites and customs.

The arrival of the Sephardic Jews was followed, in the next decades, by that of the Conversos, who were labeled *Ponentini*, those Jews who had either chosen or been forced into Christianity and were living as secret Jews in the Iberian Peninsula. Many of them who arrived in northern Italy chose to openly return to Judaism by choosing a city in which they were protected. The leading city for this was Ferrara, under the rule of the Este family. Other families who had remained Jewish throughout continued to arrive in northern Italy in this period. The famed Abrabanel family ended up in Ferrara, after initially choosing to live in the Kingdom of Naples and being uprooted again when the Kingdom, with Sicily and Sardinia, fell to the Spaniards.

Other cities had their own specific history. In Florence, for example, the Jews were protected by the Medici family, but were expelled along with them by Savonarola in 1495, later returning with the Medicis in 1533. The same held true for Rome, whose sacking by German and Spanish troops in 1527 affected the Jews as well as everyone else.

Political upheavals were sporadic, however, and generally speaking life in the Renaissance period was stable enough to allow all of the arts to flourish. The ruling princes supported scholars, artists, and writers. The thirteenth and fourteenth centuries also saw a new literary school developing among the Jews, for this was the time of Dante Alighieri (1264-1321) and his *Divine Comedy*, Petrarch (1304-1374) and his sonnets, and Boccaccio (1313-1375) with his *Decameron*. Traditional rabbinic study and creativity was also supplemented by new philosophical works, as Maimonides' writings, written in Spain and Egypt in the twelfth century, reached Italy, as did the new style of poetry from Spain, with its strong Arabic influence. Works written on science and medicine, as well as mysticism, continued to abound. But the leading writer, the poet par excellence of this period, was Immanuel of Rome (1261-1328). His *Mahberot Immanuel* is a series of 28 cantos reflecting his time with wit, obscenity, lasciviousness, and sheer genius.

> **Immanuel of Rome**
> **(c. 1261-c. 1328)**
>
> Born in Rome, Immanuel was a contemporary of Dante. Known in Italian as Manoello Giudeo ("Immanuel the Jew"), he is best known for his poetry, which he composed in both Hebrew and Italian. He moved from Rome to Perugia, and from there to Fabriano, Fermo, Ancona, Gubbio, and Verona, searching for wealthy patrons to finance his work.
>
> *Mahbarot (Compositions)* is his best known literary work, and covers all kinds of subject matter, from the frivolous to the deeply religious. There are poems on love, wine, friendship, and religious beliefs. The poem *Yigdal*, (in *Mahberet no. 4*) uses Maimonides' Thirteen Principles of Faith as its subject and is included in the Jewish prayer book (*Siddur*). His last *Mahberet* is heavily influenced by Dante's *Divine Comedy*, but has a Jewish twist.

Poetry of Immanuel of Rome

From *The Penguin Book of Hebrew Verse*, edited and translated by T. Carmi. (Great Britain: Penguin Books, 1981), 422-427 (Hebrew).

The Despicable Girl

Creative Intelligence! The day you
formed Gershom's daughter, you
shamed the universe, for in her body
you brought despicability to perfection.
You had a vile dream and
made it come true.

Perhaps you vowed to gather all disgraceful
 things together? Or you proposed
to fashion an owl and a monkey? How
did you ever dream up such a dream?
Were you low-spirited or were you drunk?

Tell me, Cherub of delineation: were
your scribers or calipers stolen from
you, so that you used a winnowing
shovel in making Gershom's daughter?

Or did the stars rebel against her?
Did the Crab and the Scorpion then
Hang onto the tail end of the
Snake, as it ascended the heavens

Hurry, Messiah

Make haste, O Messiah, why are
you lingering? They are waiting for
you, tears overflowing. Their tears have
 swelled to a torrent. O Prince, every
heart and every tongue cherishes you.

Now take a thread of line in your
hands, and measure Zion, perfect in
beauty. Then her children will surpass
all others in grace, and the
oppressive enemies will be the first to
go into exile, while you will stand fast.

Arise, Messiah, ride forth today
victoriously upon a charging horse,
 harness the chariot—for
all my bones have been scattered, and
not one is intact.

But if you mean to ride on an ass, my
Lord, go back to sleep! If so, our prince and
Messiah, allow me, in good faith, to
give you advice: keep
the end secret and seal up the vision!

a. YIGDAL

[inspired by the 13 Beliefs as listed by Maimonides]

The living God we praise, exalt, adore!
He was. He is. He will be evermore!
No unity like unto His can be:
Eternal, inconceivable is He.
[Translated by Alice Lucas]

He has no semblance—he is bodiless;
Beyond comparison is his holiness.
[Translated by Philip Birnbaum]

Before Creation's dawn He was the same;
The first to be, though never He began.
He is the world's and every creature's Lord;
His rule and majesty are manifest.
And through His chosen, glorious sons exprest
In prophecies that through their lips are poured.
Yet never like to Moses rose a seer,
Permitted glimpse behind the veil divine.
[Translated by Rabbi Adler]

The Torah of truth God gave to his people
Through his prophet, his own faithful servant.
God will never replace, nor ever change
His eternal Law for any other law.
[Translated by Birnbaum]

He observes and knows our secret heart
He sees end results at their start.
A pious man is rewarded for goodness,
An evil man for his wickedness.
[Translated by Sara Reguer]

He at the last will His anointed send,
Those to redeem, who hope, and wait the end.
God will the dead to life again restore.
Praised by His glorious name for evermore!
[Translated by Alice Lucas]

This immodesty is in stark contrast to his contemporaneous religious poetry of great refinement, such as the "*Yigdal*" of Canto 4, which reflects Maimonides' "Thirteen Principles of Faith." In a tribute to his inspiration, Immanuel's last Canto takes the reader on a trip to hell and heaven, but, unlike in Dante's work, the majority of the people the reader meets are Jewish or connected to Jewish history.

Imitating the princes, Jewish loan-bankers supported scholars and subsidized literature. They found the best teachers for their children—both boys and girls—who studied a broad curriculum while at the same time continuing their Jewish studies. We find Jewish musicians, composers, and singers, and even Jewish dance masters. Theater developed, based on the traditional Jewish Purim plays and Hanukah performances. Jews were not very active in the visual arts because most of them were produced for the Church; however, they continued to produce works of art in the fields of goldsmithing and silversmithing. They were also productive in the area of material culture, creating beautiful ritual objects like Torah mantles and covers for the Holy Ark. Some entrepreneurs started new fields, such as Anna the Hebrew, who provided expensive cosmetics for Catherine Sforza and Queen Elizabeth I. Jews also continued to shine in the traditional field of medicine.

Like their Christian neighbors, the upper- and middle-class Jews appreciated beauty. They had leisure time, which was filled with entertainment such as reading for pleasure, playing sports including tennis, hunting, and gambling with dice. Food preparation received great attention, as did the latest dress fashions for both men and women. For some, this lifestyle brought moral laxity, and the sources reflect the inability of the rabbis to curb this tendency.

Jewish women had traditionally been active in the economic sphere, and they expanded their activities in this time period. Some became physicians, others professional singers. Their education was similar to that of boys and men, and some even moved into the traditional male preserve of higher Jewish learning, the most outstanding of these were Pomona da Modena of Ferrara, and Fioretta da Modena. They were scribes, printers, and even ritual slaughterers. Two women—both of Sephardic origin—even played important roles in public life: Benvenida Abrabanel and Dona Gracia Nasi.

Anna the Hebrew (Rome)
to Catherine Sforza (Forli), 1508

Most illustrious Madonna, I send you greetings.

Messer Antonio Melozo Cavaleri was here on behalf of your illustrious Highness asking me to give him any sort of cream that would smooth the face.

First, I gave him a black cream which removes any roughness of the face, and makes the flesh smooth and supple. Put this cream on at night, and let it remain on till the morning. Then wash yourself with pure river water. Next moisten your face in the lotion that is called *Acqua da Canicare*. Then put on a dab of this white ointment; and then take less than a chickpea grain of this powder, dissolve it in the lotion called *Acqua Dolce* and put it on your face, applied very thin.

The black cream costs four *carlini* an ounce; the *Acqua da Canicare*, four *carlini* a small bottle. The ointment, that is the white cream, costs eight *carlini* an ounce; the powder, one gold ducat an ounce, and the *Acqua Dolce* will cost you a gold ducat for a small bottle.

Now if your most illustrious Highness will apply these things, I am quite sure that you will order more from us.

I commend myself to your Highness always.

Rome, the 15th of March, 1508.

Your Highness's servant
Anna the Hebrew

[P.S.] The black cream is bitter. If it should happen to go into the mouth, you may be assured that it is nothing dangerous; the bitterness comes from the aloes in it. (Pasolini, Pier Desiderio, *Caterina Sforza* Vol. III [Rome, 1893], 608-9.)

The revival of the classical languages included Hebrew, for one of the most important characteristics of a humanist was a skill in languages. Hebrew was taught in various universities. Giovanni Pico della Mirandola (1463-1494), the famous Florentine philosopher, for example, studied Hebrew with three Jewish scholars, but he did so in order to understand *Kabbala* and to use it to further his understanding of Christianity. Della Mirandola and a small, influential group of Christian scholars, in an unprecedented step, delved into Jewish texts in an attempt to understand more deeply their own spiritual roots. He and his group arrived at the concept that a single truth crossed all ages and cultures. This universalizing of religion led to a more tolerant Christian theology, with an appreciation of the contribution of Judaism to western civilization. He thought that the true source of this was *Kabbala*, which he Christianized. *Kabbala* in Renaissance Italy was unlike the *Kabbala* that traveled from Spain to Safed in the Land of Israel, where Rabbi Isaac Luria, known as the ARI, and his main disciple

Hayim Vital of Calabria, reshaped it. According to Della Mirandola, the *Kabbala* was part of ancient wisdom, and could be philosophized about and absorbed by European culture.

Another scholar who studied Hebrew in Italy was Johannes Reuchlin, who had Ovadiah Sforno (1470-1550) as his teacher. Upon returning to Germany, he became a defender of the Jews, and his studies gave him a basis for what became the Reformation. However, the Jewish contribution to humanistic writing was not fundamental, and the influence was mainly directed from the larger world to the Jewish one. Before embracing Humanism, Jews had to come up with a rationale for moving away from traditional Jewish-centered learning. They did so, in part, by deciding that all learning was already in the Bible and that by participating in humanistic endeavors Jews were recovering Biblical wisdom. Influenced by the books on Greek and Latin grammar that were being written, a new grammar of Biblical Hebrew was created in 1403 by Profiat Duran to help not only scholars but all educated Jews.

> **Ovadiah Sforno**
> **(ca. 1470-ca. 1550)**
>
> Born in Cesena, Italy, near Ravenna, Ovadiah Sforno studied in Rome where is mastered medicine, Hebrew philology, and traditional Jewish studies. On Cardinal Grimani's recommendation he taught Hebrew to the Christian humanist Johannes Reuchlin.
> Settling in Bologna, where he helped revive the Jewish community, Ovadiah Sforno also played an active role in reviving a Hebrew printing house in that city. Best known for his commentary on the Torah and a selection of books from the Prophets and Writings, he stressed contemporary scientific explanations and humanistic ideas along with literal exegesis.

The Jews were part of the universal intellectual curiosity of the Renaissance, but they also picked up some of its immorality, and engaged in activities such as card playing, gambling, enjoying hedonism, and sexual misdeeds.

A prime example of the positive side of this era was Judah Messer Leon, a doctor, rabbinic scholar, and philosopher living in Mantua. He studied the humanities, but found Jewish origins for admired virtues. For example, in his "*Nofet Tsufim*," he portrayed the humanist image of leadership as a man obliged to lead his community by virtue of a unique combination of learning plus good character, and the first examples of this—including the use of the art of rhetoric—predated Greece and Rome, for they were the Prophets of ancient Israel.

Alongside the traditional Jewish field of Talmudic study, the Renaissance period saw the expansion of Jewish interests into poetry, linguistics, homiletics, history, biography, geography, and philosophy. Hebrew poetry was influenced by Italian forms and covered a multiplicity of topics, from religious hymns to love songs to epics. All of these fields of study were aided by the new technology of printing. Technology had been developing for centuries when Johann Gutenberg (1398-1468) is said to have combined all that he had learned from his forefathers and created the printing press. These technologies combined the mechanics of wine and olive presses, knowledge of inks and metallurgy, and the technology of paper making. The press itself had to combine physics and mechanics to use enough pressure on the paper so that the ink remained, but not so much as to ruin the paper. The ink must not fade, and the metals used for the movable type must be soft enough to withstand the pressure of a press. The paper must be thick enough to be printed on both sides, and be of a quality such that it would not be acidic enough to fade with time. Gutenberg combined the knowledge of centuries, and used the form of moveable type that worked best for him. Perhaps Guttenberg's only new discovery was the use of alum, the final element needed to make the ink dry rapidly. He used wet paper when printing (which had never been done

Judah Messer Leon

An Italian rabbi, physician and philosopher, Judah Messer Leon was born in the province of Vicenza. Also known as Yehudah ben Yehiel Rofe, he was educated in both secular and religious studies. He was given the honorific title "Messer" (a title of knighthood) by the Emperor Frederick III in 1452, perhaps for his work as the emperor's physician.

Settling in Ancona, Judah Messer Leon set up a *Yeshiva* in which traditional Jewish education was combined with the secular curriculum of the time. This *Yeshiva* followed him when he moved to Padua, Bologna, Mantua, and finally Naples.

Judah Messer Leon wrote in the scholastic style, addressing the Renaissance stress on grammar, logic, and rhetoric, the *trivium* then seen as the prerequisites for higher studies in the humanities, medicine, and philosophy. His most famous work, *Sefer Nofet Tzufim (The Book of the Honeycomb's Flow)*, was written in Hebrew using the new genre of rhetorical writing. Integrating philosophy and rhetoric, he set forth the new image of the Jewish leader as a person obliged to lead the community by virtue of a combination of broad and substantive learning plus good character. He demonstrated to non-Jews that the model of oratory was not Greece nor Rome, but the prophets of ancient Israel.

before) and added alum, which was first used in the mixing of Dutch oil paints, to the ink. This allowed for the possibility of printing on both sides of the page.

The first Hebrew book was probably published in Rome ca.1468, and it was in Italy that the art of the Hebrew book flourished. Here was a stable Jewish community, with the education, the leisure time, and the money necessary to give the impetus needed to support this new endeavor. The audience for Hebrew books included wealthy and middle class men, and also the women of their families, who were usually literate in Hebrew.

The Jews probably came into contact with the predominantly Christian technology of printing at the international book fairs, towns

---

The Printing of Gershom Soncino

… [Printed] by me, Gershom Soncino, son of the sage, Rabbi Moshe son of the sage Rabbi Israel Natan…. In the twelfth year of the mighty king, our lord the Sultan Suleyman, may his Majesty be exalted, in Constantinople. Printed with vocalization and with references … and I correct the copyists' errors….

May He, the blessed One, allow His splendor to radiate on he who waits and hopes for His love, and may He guide me in His truth and teach me, even as He has led me from strength to strength since my youth. I worked to discover books that had been stored and hidden away for a long time, and I brought them into the light of the sun, and they shine like the radiance of heaven: namely the *Tosafot* of Rabbi Isaac and Rabbenu Tam. I went as far as France and Chambery and Geneva, to the very places where these writings were conceived, in order to give the public the benefit of them….

I published innumerable books dealing with our holy Torah, as well as twenty-three Talmudic tractates, which are commonly studied in the academies, with the Rashi commentary and the *Tosafot.* The Venetian printers copied my books and published, in addition, whatever they could lay their hands on. They tried hard to ruin me, but thus far God has helped me. And, although time the deceiver has played havoc with me, while there is yet breath in my body I shall not cease to issue good editions in order to lighten the burdens of those who read them and to illumine their darkness, if only God will be with me….

May God help me and support my old age and remember that I supported the Conversos of Spain and Portugal, and with all my might, even in extreme danger, I tried to save them from their enemies and to lead them back to God….

Blessed be the name of Him who is forever to be praised. (Gershom Soncino, Title Page for his printing of David Kimchi's *Mikhlol,* [Constantinople: 1534.])

where printers, booksellers, and publishers met and made transactions. Since moneychangers were also present, and many were Jews, this may be how the word spread of the new technology of printing.

The first Hebrew book printed in Italy was the *Mishne Torah* of Maimonides, which was printed outside Rome by two monks between 1468 and 1470. Presses opened in other cities; for example a man named Conat and his wife Estellina owned one in Mantua, and Abraham ben Hayim the Dyer had one in Bologna. The most famous Jewish printers were of the family of Soncino, who originated in Germany. The most famous member of this family was Gershom son of Moses Soncino (d.1534) who traveled all over Italy with his type, press, and woodcuts. The Soncino family produced over half of the Hebrew *incunabula* (books printed before 1500), including editions of most of the volumes of Talmud, a complete Bible with diacritical marks, and a Mahzor according to the Roman rite which served to unify Jews of Italian origin. Gershom was also interested in secular Hebrew works and printed *Mashal ha-Qadmoni* and poetry of Immanuel of Rome. But the printer who produced the entire Talmud was not a Jew: Daniel Bomberg set up his printing press in Venice, a city that forbade Jews from participating in the printing profession, and printed a uniform twenty-three volume Talmud between 1519 and 1523. However, even the field of printing saw major competition, and

---

Gershom Soncino
(ca. 1460s-1534)

Gershom Soncino was born into the family of Hebrew printers which took its name from the city of Soncino, near Cremona, where they had settled after obtaining permission from Francesco Sforza, duke of Milan, in 1454. Gershom was one of the most successful printers of his time, printing from 1489 to 1534 works in Hebrew, Latin, Greek, and Italian. In non-Hebrew works he used the names Hieronymus [Latin] or Geronimo [Italian].

Gershom Soncino traveled from city to city because of local political conditions and fierce competition. He printed in Soncino, Casalmaggiore, Brescia, Barco, Fano, Pesaro, Rimini, and Ancona. He published Hebrew manuscripts, was the first to use woodcut illustrations for a Hebrew work, printed the secular Hebrew poetry of Immanuel of Rome, and also printed books in a small pocket-size format. His typeface was aesthetically beautiful, as were his books.

Towards the end of his life he left Italy for Turkey, continuing to print in Salonika and Istanbul.

the fights between printers ended in Papal censorship and even in the burning of Hebrew books, starting in 1553 in Rome. The Inquisition had investigated and had condemned the Talmud as an anti-Christian work. This was part of the Catholic Church's attempt to meet the challenge of the Protestant Reformation.

**Burning of the Talmud in Italy,
from *Emek ha-Bakha* by Joseph ha-Cohen**

In those days certain evil men emerged from our midst and accused things that were not true against the Torah of the Lord our God, and stiffened their necks and sinned against the Lord. They despised the covenant which God had made with our fathers and followed the Gentiles, about whom the Lord had commanded that they should not imitate. They provoked Him very much with their vanities and continued to sin.

They brought an evil report against the Talmud to the Pope [Julius III], saying: "There is a certain Talmud widely spread among the Jews and its laws differ from those of all peoples. It curses your Messiah and it ill befits the Pope to tolerate it." He became very angry and his fury raged within him and he said: "Remove it and let it be burnt." No sooner had the command left his lips than the officers went forth, rushing out in haste, and entered the houses of the Jews and brought the books found there into the city-square and burnt them on the Sabbath day, on the festival of New Year in the year 5314, that is, 1553. And the children of Israel cried over the burning which the enemies of God had lit.

These are the names of those informers who stirred up our troubles: Hananel da Foligno, Joseph Moro, Shlomo Romano. O Lord, do not blot out their sin but deal with them in the time of your anger.

Fleet messengers went forth to the anointed and tonsured people throughout Romagna so that in Bologna and Ravenna innumerable books were burnt on the Sabbath, and the children of Israel sighed and cried aloud but they had no power to help themselves. In Ferrara and Mantua, too, the books were burnt by order of the Pope who commanded that they were to be destroyed.... In Venice, too, they sought to lay their hands even on the Torah scrolls in the ark, but the congregational heads stood in the breach and saved them from their hands.

And in all the rest of the places to which the command of the Pope reached, there was great mourning among the Jews and fasting and weeping and wailing.... In the Duchies of Milan and Montferrat they did not follow the command of the Pope who was odious to Don Ferrante [Gonzaga], the Viceroy...

The community leaders went to the Pope and he received them graciously in that he allowed them to keep the works of the later lawmakers, so as to leave them a remnant in the land, but he would not listen to them with respect to the books of the Talmud.... (Joseph ha-Cohen, *Emek ha-Bakha*. Jerusalem: Lewin-Epstein, 1957.)

Title page of Bible
printed by Gershom Soncino
in Soncino, 1488
(R. Fodde collection and photograph)

Love of the book is reflected in the traditional field of rabbinic literature. There were Ashkenazi *yeshivot* in the north of Italy, most notably the ones headed by Rabbi Joseph Colon and Rabbi Judah Minz of Padua. Verona and Cremona also had *yeshivot*. However, the Italian *yehivot* also taught secular studies, and were geared to both young men and adult scholars. Rabbinic literature consisted mainly of collections of laws and customs, and the main form of religious guidance continued to be the *Responsa*. These are often stylistic masterpieces of individualism. Much has been written on the intellectual, institutional, and social aspects of the rabbinate in Italy during this period of time; see particularly the recommended reading for this chapter.

After the Church banned both the printing and the owning of the Talmud in the mid-sixteenth century, the rabbis used substitute works, especially *Sefer ha-Halakhot* by Rabbi Isaac Alfassi, because he quoted so much Talmud in it. But there is no question that this ban was a blow to Judaism and learning.

An interesting creative outlet for the rabbis was preaching, and although their sermons were delivered in Italian to an audience that included Christians, they were written in Hebrew. Some books of these sermons survived, and many reflect the influence of Humanism as well as the moral failings of some members of the community.

The Renaissance period is the focus of much interest from students of many fields of scholarship. The personalities of the figures involved alone attract much attention, setting aside the art, culture, and political and economic rivalries. Scholars of Jewish intellectual history, studying the enormous output of all types of thought during this era, wrestle with some basic questions, such as: did the cultural world of the Christians influence the way Jews thought about their Judaism? Was there any contribution from Jewish intellectuals to the Renaissance itself? If the Jewish intellectuals were forced to rethink their Judaism, did this lessen their attachment to their traditions?

Most scholars agree that there was a relative openness of cultural exchange both with other Jewish communities and with Christians. While they had received traditional Jewish educations, the interest of most Jewish intellectuals was not in *halakhic* matters but in Jewish thought as it paralleled Renaissance thought. Jewish scholars moved about from country to country, came to the cities of northern Italy, and met other Jewish scholars in the synagogues or homes of wealthy Jewish patrons of culture. Jewish doctors, who were often rabbis as well, and Converso physicians helped shape Jewish culture too, and the Jewish graduates of the universities kept in touch over the years. Rabbis continued to play an intellectual role, as they mostly sought to balance the Humanistic ideas of the age with their religious beliefs. Some, however, did become more culturally ambivalent.

Italian Jews, according to the latest scholarship, did play a real role in shaping Jewish intellectual life in early modern Europe. They integrated

> **Elijah Delmedigo**
> **(ca. 1458-ca. 1497)**
>
> Born in Candia, Crete, Delmedigo had a traditional Jewish education, also studying philosophy, Arabic, Greek, and Latin. Moving to Padua, one of the important centers of Aristotelian philosophy in Italy, he became a leading authority on Averroes, the Arab commentator on Aristotle, teaching his ideas there, in Venice, and in Perugia. In this last city he met Pico Della Mirandola, who studied with him. Another Christian student was Domenico Grimani, soon to become Cardinal of San Marco. Both became his patrons, but Delmedigo disagreed with the intellectual path taken by them. In addition, he differed with the Italian Jewish community over a number of issues, and so decided to return to Crete. There he wrote his major work, *Sefer Behinat ha-Dat (Examination of Faith)*, completing it in 1490. It is a major work of Jewish philosophy, discussing, among many other things, the boundaries of philosophy and religious faith.

and reinterpreted Jewish thought as a result of being part of the cultural life of the Christian Renaissance. They learned how to translate and transmit their culture into the larger world, as is seen most clearly in the court of Pico Della Mirandola in Florence, and in the emergence of the Christian Hebraists. However, one must keep in mind that the mentality of the time was such that Jews always viewed the world through Jewish lenses. Their days were measured by Jewish time, on a daily level by the schedule for prayers, and on an annual level by the Jewish calendar. The synagogue was used not only as a sacred space but also for community needs, such as study, justice, and cycle of life ceremonies such as circumcisions, weddings, divorces, and sometimes eulogies. And while Jews spoke Italian and their clothing and foods were influenced by their neighbors, the Jews were never accepted as equals by their Christian neighbors, nor could they be, because religion was *the* dividing line. It was this collective awareness of being different that colored everything else.

Recommended Reading

Bonfil, Roberto. *Jewish Life in Renaissance Italy.* Los Angeles: University of California Press, 1994.

David, Robert C., & Benjamin Ravid, eds. *The Jews of Early Modern Venice.* Baltimore: Johns Hopkins University Press, 2001.

Ruderman, David B. *Essential Papers on Jewish Culture in Renaissance and Baroque Italy.* New York: NYU Press, 1992.

Shulvass, Moses A. *The Jews in the World of the Renaissance.* Leiden: Brill, 1973.

Zeldes, Nadia. "The Former Jews of this Kingdom", in *Sicilian Converts after the Expulsion, 1402-1516.* Leiden: Brill, 2003.

Timeline

GENERAL		JEWISH
	1437	Florence Jewish community starts
	1492	Spanish Expulsion of Jews
	1516	Ghetto Nuovo in Venice
Martin Luther begins Reformation	1517	
	1510—1569	Dona Gracia Nasi
Inquisition in Italy	1542	
Ignatius Loyola	1543	First Casa dei Catecumenei, Rome
	1547	Expulsion from Kingdom of Naples
Cosimo dei Medici	1537—1574	
Pope Paul IV *Cum Nimis Absurdum*	1555	Ghetto in Rome
Ferdinando I Medici	1587—1609	Building of Livorno
	c. 1592—1641	Sara Coppio Sullam
Index	1564	
	1571	Ghetto in Florence
	1593	Livorniana
	1571—1648	Leone da Modena
	1570—1630	Salomone de' Rossi
	1665/6	Shabbtai Zvi the False Messiah
	1697	Ghetto in Trieste
Trieste declared a free port by Habsburg Empire	1707—1747	R. Moses Hayim Luzzatto
Emperor Joseph II of Habsburg Empire	1781/2	Edict of Toleration – Trieste
French Revolution	1789	

Chapter 5

The Ghetto

The period of the Renaissance ushers in an abundance of primary sources on the Jews of Italy. We not only have church documents of all sorts, but we also now have a plethora of government documents ranging from permissions to settle in a given city to very specific contracts for opening loan banks. Jewish sources include religious tracts as well as works of secular poetry, literature, philosophy, science, and even Hebrew grammar. Community records have survived, including records of court cases, as well as some synagogue architecture and cemeteries. Thus we can carefully follow the re-creation of communities north of the Papal States, sometimes in great detail.

Each Jewish community in the north is typically Italian-Jewish, while at the same time exhibiting its own unique features. In each of them, the Jews argued for permission to reside based on the utilitarian economic needs of the city. Each city was ruled by a different prince, and each prince had a different attitude to the Pope as well as to the Jews. Politics was a constant game played out within economic and religious contexts. The Jews reflected the uniqueness of their cities, while they were also involved in similar survival needs. Thus they all built synagogues, focused on education, and tried to earn livings to support their families. Each Jewish community's identity was also complicated by the ethnicity of its members, who were constantly migrating and adding to the Italian mix. We will examine only the outstanding communities of this period, specifically those of Venice, Florence, Livorno, Rome, and Trieste.

The most outstanding example is Venice, the name of whose Jewish area of settlement came to represent all Jewish neighborhoods for historians, whether residence in the Jewish neighborhood was forced or voluntary: the "ghetto." While Venice's was not the first forcibly segregated and enclosed Jewish quarter in Europe, its name became the norm.

In their move north, Jews began to reside in cities of the Venetian territories, such as Padua, Verona, and Mestre, which is just across the water from present-day Venice. When the League of Cambrai armies invaded in 1509, as part of the European monarchs' power struggle, the Jews of Mestre fled across the lagoon to Venice. This small Jewish community was typical for its time, and was centered around the families of loan bankers. Initially opposed to allowing Jews in to the city, the Venetian government soon realized that there were economic benefits in granting permission, for not only was there a need for the urban middle class and the poor to borrow relatively small sums of money, but the Jews could also be required to pay the city a heavy tax for the privilege of residence. In a society that included a large stratum of craftspeople, peasants, and small traders, who usually had no savings, there was a constant need for money loans to tide people over during an illness, or to help them buy seed or raw materials. Venice did not have two other popular categories of borrowers, namely university students and unpaid soldiers, but there were always the temporarily monetarily embarrassed professionals, shopkeepers, clergy, and merchants. Jewish loan bankers could lend money on the security of pawns, promissory notes, and even land.

As the Venetian government argued over whether or not to allow in these loan bankers, a great incentive was the money to be made not only from the renewable *condotta*, but also from the taxes on each loan. There was also the intriguing availability of a loan for urgent events like raising

Bridge leading to the Ghetto of Venice, first enclosed in 1516
(R. Fodde photograph)

money for troops to be considered. The argument against allowing Jews in was based on the practical fear of economic rivalry and the Christian fear of "contamination," as well as the Christian law against usury.

The compromise that was reached was to allow loan bankers and their families to settle in Venice, but they had to be segregated in an enclosed space in rented quarters. The most practical space was that of the old copper *ghetto*, or foundry, which had produced both copper and bronze weapons of war but no longer did so. The tons of metallic waste dumped by the foundry had gradually resulted in a stable island, around which walls were erected. Gates were built, and they were locked at night by guards. This *Ghetto Nuovo*, or "New Ghetto" (to differentiate it from the old foundry itself or *Ghetto Vecchio*), became the Jewish quarter starting in 1516.

Originally the ghetto gates were closed at sunset, but the hours were extended until later during the winter months, probably because it got dark earlier. Only Jewish doctors treating important sick Christians, and rich Jewish merchants who had to see to their business, were allowed outside of the gates after hours. Occasionally this privilege was given to individuals who had special skills, such as singers and dancers who performed at Carnival time.

The loan bankers were joined by a group of Jews dealing in secondhand goods, especially clothing and household items, which included furnishings. By this time, second hand goods dealers and loan bankers were among the only professions open to Italian and German Jews, who were lumped together under the rubric *Tedeschi.*

The Jews moving into the *Ghetto Nuovo* had to figure out how to best use the space allotted to them. Central to it was a large square or *piazza,* fringed by two- or three-story houses. The buildings were not of the best quality. The space had to be divided into living quarters, shops, stalls, storerooms, and workrooms. Even though the buildings were rented, the Jews subdivided the apartments and also built upward. New entryways were added, as were passageways and quays. After a few decades, the *Ghetto Nuovo* was a maze that could be traversed only by the knowledgeable. The overcrowded conditions presented challenges for hygiene, cleanliness, and access to clean water—challenges successfully met by the Jewish community.

A different challenge presented itself to the *Tedeschi* Jews when the Venetian government changed its attitude toward Jews in international trade. With the changing political and economic realities of the sixteenth century, Venice wanted to cultivate trade with the Ottoman Empire, so as to compete with other rival Italian city-states. The *Levantini* Jews were thus invited in. These included Middle Eastern Jews of the Ottoman Empire and Sephardic Jews who had fled the Iberian Peninsula after 1492, settling in places like Istanbul and Salonika. Some were wealthy international traders who even had influence in the Ottoman Turkish court, and they refused to move into the *Ghetto Nuovo.* After much debate, the Venetian government, insistent that these too were "detestable" Jews who had to be segregated from Christians, gave them the *Ghetto Vecchio,* where the foundry had been torn down, granting them room to build relatively large quarters for their families. These new arrivals followed Sephardic rite and customs, and so quickly founded their own synagogue and community structure.

The third group of Jews to arrive was a potentially dangerous one for the Venetian government. These were *Conversos,* or New Christians, from Spain and Portugal, many of whom returned to Judaism when it was safe to do so. The neutral term created for this group was *Ponentini* or "Western Jews." Economically they were equal to the *Levantini,* but they wanted their own space, hence the *Ghetto Nuovissimo* of 1633. Until then most had been living as Christians outside the ghetto. It was an open secret that many *Ponentini* were Judaizers, yet out of the thousands of hearings held by the Inquisition in Venice between 1541 and 1794, fewer than five percent dealt with Judaizing or Jews. We may therefore assume that Venice was a relatively safe place for *Conversos*, despite its anti-Jewish sentiments.

Thus there were three discrete Jewish ethnic communities, each arriving in Venice at a different time, and each making different arrangements with the Venetian government and living in separate ghettos, connected by bridges. Yet despite the many differences, the three groups had to cooperate in a Jewish self-government within what became the unified ghetto. A main reason for the necessity of this inter-community cooperation was precisely what made the Venetian ghetto unique: instead of each individual loan banker being responsible for the tax paid to the government, by 1598 this became a collective responsibility.

The *Universita,* or self-government system of the Jews, consisted of a Large Assembly which was made up of all the Jews who fit the criteria of gender, age, and wealth. This body elected a Small Assembly, which managed most of the affairs of the community, including municipal services like sanitation, fire-fighting, and crime-prevention. The three ethnic groups were constantly vying for power, so they developed intricate procedures to ensure equality.

The Small Assembly ran the day-to-day government of the ghetto. The number of men serving varied from seven to thirteen. Aiding the Small Assembly were committees, the most important of which were the banking committee and the assessment committee. No one wanted to serve on the latter, because these were the men who determined how much a man had to pay toward the government tax as well as toward the community tax.

Being a member of the Small Assembly was a demanding responsibility in part because the members of the committee would have to pay out of their own pockets if not enough money was raised for city demands. Their responsibilities included passing rules to implement municipal laws, representing individual Jews before the municipal government, fulfilling municipal tasks, and providing Jewish leadership in cooperation with the rabbis. This last responsibility included things like supervising the provision of kosher meat and the baking of *matza* and enforcing the sumptuary laws. The rabbis seem not to have played an important official role in the ghetto's political life, but their influence was powerful; they enforced communal decisions by persuasion, using the ultimate threat of excommunication.

Sara Coppio Sullam
(ca. 1592-1641)

The product of a liberal education, Sara Coppio was fluent in Hebrew, Italian, Greek, and Latin. Rising to join the ranks of the outstanding Italian poets, she is also reputed to have been an excellent musician. When she married Jacob Sullam, a rich and cultured Venetian Jew, their home became a salon where distinguished Jewish and Christian intellectuals and literary figures met. Inspired by his correspondence with her, the Italian poet Ansaldo Ceba attempted to persuade her to convert to Christianity. Another Christian, the priest Baldassar Bonifaccio [later Bishop of Capodistria], publicly denounced her in a published pamphlet, accusing her of not believing in the immortality of the soul, a charge that could have led to action by the Inquisition. Sara Coppio Sullam responded to both with great erudition and conviction, reflecting her deep devotion to Judaism.

The Small Assembly's main tool of enforcement was a monetary fine for noncompliance, which was enforced by the Venetian municipal powers.

This internal government was not a democracy, but more of an oligarchy. Within such a male-dominated system there is not much material on the lives of women, nor on members of the lower classes, made up of craftspeople, petty business people, and laborers. There were some outstanding female personalities who lived in Venice, such as Sara Coppio Sullam (ca. 1592-1641), and Beatrice Benveniste de Luna, also known as Dona Gracia Nasi (1510-1569), who briefly resided there. What we do know is that there were many women with wealth, which they obtained either through dowries or through bequests in wills. This wealth included money, jewelry, and residential rights in properties. Women were educated, but not to the same level as their brothers. Their lives were centered on the family and on charitable activities for the community.

Like all Jewish communities, the Venetian ghetto organized *hevrot*, or pious confraternities, to see to the needs of the less fortunate. The first was the *Gemilut Hasadim* society, which cared for the dead. The issue of where to bury the Jewish dead was addressed at the beginning of ghetto life, for there was to be no Jewish cemetery in Venice itself. At first the Jews buried their dead on the mainland, and then they acquired a separate small island to serve as a cemetery. Another society was dedicated to supplying money, food, and firewood to the poor. A third devoted itself to providing dowries for brides. Another was purely devotional. Everyone knew everyone, and so all of the Jewish community's needs were met.

Dona Gracia (Mendes) Nasi (1510-ca. 1569)

Born into a Converso family in Portugal, Dona Gracia married into the Mendes family, one of the wealthiest Converso families there. Widowed at a young age, Dona Gracia took over her husband's position in the family's international trading business until she fled with her daughter, first to Antwerp and then to Venice, to escape Christian suitors interested in marrying her daughter. In Venice, she openly returned to Judaism, moving to Ferrara, which was safer for such Jews. During her four years there, she involved herself in the Spanish translation of the Bible which was printed in 1554 and is known as "The Ferrara Bible." This project was created to aid Spanish-speaking Conversos in Iberia to retain access to the source of Judaism.

Moving once again, now to escape the Inquisition, Dona Gracia ended up in Istanbul, where she used her influence and wealth to build schools, synagogues, and hospitals. She remained actively involved in a Converso "underground railroad," and in aiding fellow Conversos, such as those arrested by the Inquisiton in Ancona, the eastern port of the Papal States. She also tried to help the Jews of Safed become economically self-sufficient by encouraging the creation of a manufacturing center in Tiberias. Her nephew and heir, Don Joseph Nasi, married her daughter and carried on her work.

Education for Jews of the ghetto depended on wealth. Most boys and men were literate, and sons of rabbis were well educated in traditional Jewish studies, but only the wealthy could afford the tutors who taught the latest in the arts, literature, and science. Printing made more books available to more people, and Venice as a whole was alive with the most up-to-date publications, for scholars and authors came from all over Europe to have their works printed in one of the excellent printing houses available. They exchanged ideas and influenced each other, and the Venetian Jews were not left out of this Renaissance humanistic ferment. The art of preaching in synagogues spread these new ideas to a wider, mixed audience. The synagogue was also the stage for the new musical culture of polyphonic choral music espoused by the multi-talented Rabbi Leone da Modena and composed by Salomone de' Rossi of Mantua.

Remarkably, Venice allowed Jews to attend the University of Padua, which at the time was within Venetian territory. Jews from all over Europe came to Padua to take classes in the liberal arts and sciences, many taking their degrees in medicine. Medicine had been a respected Jewish profession for centuries, but another factor attracted Jews to this field: Renaissance thinkers separated science from religion and metaphysics, enabling Jews to be comfortable in their studies, as there was no threat to their religious beliefs. Jewish doctors exchanged ideas with each other as well as with Christians, and the connections continued well after graduation. One outstanding student was Tobias Cohen (1652-1729), who came to Padua from Germany. He wrote *Maʾase Tuvia,* which was printed in 1707 and became the most important Hebrew medical book of its time. However, he ended up practicing medicine in the much more welcoming climate of the Ottoman Empire.

With the economic decline of Venice in the eighteenth century, Jewish economic life in the ghetto also declined, as did the population figures. The Venetian Jewish community only revived in the modern period, and when it did reestablish itself, it appeared in a very different form than that of the protected yet despised "other" of the late Renaissance and early modern periods.

The Jewish community of Florence, as was typical of northern Jewish communities, began with an invitation, in 1437, to a Jewish loan banker. Gradually the wealthy merchants began to arrive, but the majority of the Jews of Florence were smaller merchants and artisans, who surprisingly managed to be accepted into the guilds dealing with wool, silk, and linen; there were also a number of doctors and pharmacists. Jews lived in a number of Tuscan cities and towns, and numbered only about 700 people; this number grew after 1569 from the flow of Jews northward from the Papal States.

Throughout the sixteenth century, there was intense international trade rivalry between the Ottoman Empire and Europe, as well as among the various European countries trying to obtain trade footholds in the Ottoman Empire. The Balkans trade expanded, and the Italian city-states faced new competition from Western European countries, each trying to carve out commercial niches for itself.

Many of the Jews of the Ottoman Empire had moved, over the centuries, into commerce, which did not interest the Ottoman Turks. The Ottoman Jews had the advantages of knowing multiple languages, having international ties, and being a "neutral" party between Muslims and Christians. With the Spanish Expulsion of the Jews in 1492, a sizeable number of Sephardim made their way to the Ottoman Empire, bringing

Letter of Leone da Modena (1571-1648)
to the Jewish Public, Venice, 1623

... It is from the Hebrews that the other nations have borrowed music. Who could forget an aging King David, that wonderful poet, who taught the sons of Asaph music, as it is written? ... while instrumental music flourished during the long period of the first and the second Temples.

But our banishment, our dispersal over the earth ... caused inevitably the decline and downfall of the arts. For when the anger of the Lord fell upon us, nothing was left of our spiritual wealth.... We have been compelled to borrow our music from other nations and to adapt it to our religious songs; until this era when Solomon made his appearance [i.e., Salomone de Rossi], who excelled in the musical science not only among the Jews but also among the non-Jews. He is part of the choir of the Duke of Mantua.... His musical works composed for Italian texts were so successful that many of them have been received with admiration everywhere. His music has been so praised that we might say: "God has opened the eyes of the blind and unstopped the ears of the deaf." He also turned faithfully to the Lord, and each day added Psalms, hymns and synagogal songs to those of the previous day. He has collected them into one volume. Now his followers are eager to sing his compositions....

The heads of the community, above all the revered and virtuous Moses Sullam—may God bless him—urged the author to publish his compositions.... I, too, who am proud to be counted among his friends, used all my influence to convince him to publish his work. At last he yielded to our biddings and delivered his collection to the printer under the patronage of the generous Moses Sullam.... He entrusted to me the supervision of the printing, and the revision and correction of errors. Unfortunately ... my heart was cruelly torn by the death of my son Zebulun, may he rest in peace, a youth of twenty-one, on whom were built the finest hopes, and endowed with great musical talent, who was murdered by his co-religionists six months ago. My soul rejects any consolation, and will never hear music again. Yet I did not want to delay any longer this work which I had agreed to perform.... I have, therefore, resumed my work again....

Attached here is an important document, the answer to a question which was put before me when I was rabbi in Ferrara. My answer, which has been endorsed by all the great rabbis of Venice, was complete proof that nothing in the Talmud forbids the introduction of choral singing into our synagogues. This may close the malignant mouths of the opponents... I invite all our faithful Jews to cultivate song and music in our synagogues ... until the anger of Lord of Israel turns away from us, and until He restores His Temple in Zion, where the Levites will again sing their songs of joy, in another manner than today.... (Salomone De Rossi, *Ha-Shirim Asher Li-Shlomo* [Venice: 1623]).

Salomone de'Rossi
(ca. 1570-1630)

The leading Jewish composer of the late Italian Renaissance, Salomone de'Rossi (Shlomo *Min-ha-Adumim*) was a court musician of the Gonzagas of Mantua. He began as a singer and viola player, and advanced to become leader of an instrumental ensemble which was so well known that the duke loaned it to other courts. When Mantua was attacked by the Hapsburg army (1628-30), most of its Jewish musicians fled to Venice, where Leone da Modena sponsored them in the *'Accademia degli Impediti.'*

Salomone started as a madrigalist, but soon turned to ornamental monody, songs or instrumental pieces with one leading solo voice supported by a fundamental bass. He was the pioneer of these baroque forms. He also composed music for Hebrew texts, especially his *Ha-Shirim Asher li-Shlomo,* which was published in 1622/3, and used three to eight voices, in *a capella* style.

Leone da Modena
(1571-1648)

A product of the many-sided education of rich Jews of the Renaissance, Leone da Modena was well versed in both the traditional Jewish curriculum and the secular one, which included Italian, Latin, poetry, music, and dance. A child prodigy, Leone developed into an outstanding scholar with great intellectual versatility. During his tenure as a rabbi in Venice, his eloquent sermons attracted non-Jews, especially the educated and upper classes of Christians.

His many works include his *Historia de Riti Hebraici (History of Jewish Rites),* which was one of the first Jewish books written in a European language and geared to non-Jews. It was written in 1616 in Italian, for presentation to James I, King of England. This book reflects a new awareness by Jews and Christians of each other. But it is also a kind of social polemic, presenting a rational and moral religion with no superstitions. He justified usury within morality and described commercial ethics, all to combat stereotypes. The book was very popular all over Europe.

Leone was a prolific letter writer, leaving a wealth of details about himself and his surroundings. He also composed one of the earliest Hebrew autobiographies, *Hayyei Yehuda.*

From Leone Da Modena's *Life of Judah*

... While my heart was still full of sorrow because of the distance from my son-in-law and daughter, there came an enormous anxiety, fear, and heartache greater than anything I had experienced before among the very great number of troubles and sorrows that I had every day since I was born. About two years earlier I had given a certain Frenchman who knows the Holy Tongue ... a certain book to read. I had written it earlier at the request of an English nobleman, who was to give it to the king of England. In it I relate all the laws, doctrines, and customs of the Jews at the present time in their Diaspora. When I wrote it I was not careful about not writing things contrary to the Inquisition, because it was only in manuscript and was meant to be read by people who were not of the pope's persuasion.

After reading it, that Frenchman asked me to leave it with him and he would print it in France. I agreed, but did not think of editing out the things that the Inquisition in Italy might find unacceptable in a printed book.

Two years later, after I had given up hope that the Frenchman might print it, on the second day of Passover 5397 [1637], a man brought me a letter from him, in which he told me that he had printed the book in Paris.... My heart immediately began pounding, and I went to look at a copy of it that I still had from the time I had written it and I saw four or five things recorded of which it is forbidden to speak, much less to write, and needless to say to print, against the will of the Inquisition. Heartbroken, I shouted and tore at my beard until I almost lost my breath for I said to myself, "When this book is seen in Rome, it will become a stumbling block for all the Jews. They will say, 'How insolent are they to print in the vernacular, informing the Christians not only of their laws, but also of some matters against our religion and beliefs.'" As for me, where could I go? I could not escape to Ferrara or to any other place in Italy.... Then God, the kind and merciful, put into my mind the idea to seek the advice of the Inquisitor, may he be blessed and praised, for he had always acted like one of the righteous gentiles in his dealings with me. So I made a voluntary declaration to the Inquisition, which protected me on every count and on which I relied. Thus, after about a month of indescribably pain and sorrow, I relaxed....

Not long afterward the aforementioned Frenchman arrived in Rome, and from there he sent me a copy of the book that had been printed in Paris. I saw that he had been clever and considerate enough to delete the four or five items over which I had worried. He had also written a letter to me in the introduction, enthusiastically praising and glorifying me and my work. He dedicated the book to a nobleman, the ambassador of the king of France, who had just come here to take up residence.... (Leone Da Modena, *Leket Ktavim* [Jerusalem: Mosad Bialik, 1968], 85-87).

with them both trade and manufacturing expertise. This commercial power was perceived by Western countries as important, and the perception of Jewish power was reinforced by the role played by individual Jews in the courts of the sultans.

This combination of factors is probably what led Ferdinand I, Grand Duke of Tuscany, to invite Ottoman Jews, *Levantini*, to come to his domain in 1591. This was not the first time that the Medicis had dealt with *Levantini*, nor with their western brothers, the "Portuguese" (as they called the converts to Christianity) and the Sephardim. The Medicis, ruling from their seat of power in Florence, generally had a tolerant attitude to the Jews.

When Cosimo I de' Medici (1537-1574) ruled, he allowed Jewish loan bankers to settle where there were no *Monte di Pieta,* Christian loan banks for the poor. He welcomed Sephardic Jews, especially those of the family of Samuel Abrabanel, to settle in Tuscany after the Spanish-controlled Kingdom of Naples expelled them in 1547. Benvenida, Samuel's wife, had tutored Cosimo's wife, and personal connections were always important. Cosimo even provided a safe haven for Italian Jews escaping the Papal States after 1555, when the Pope forced the Jews of the Papal States into ghettos. But Cosimo carefully balanced his role as a secular ruler with his identity as a good Catholic, and so the "Portuguese," or converts, had to live as Christians while residing in Florence. The charter granted to them in 1549 gave them monopolies in the trades of Spanish wool, a special red dye, pearls, sugar, pepper, and silk. In 1551, he went so far as to invite merchants of the Ottoman Empire in

> **Benvenida Abrabanel**
> **(ca. 1480s–ca.1560s)**
>
> Married to her cousin Samuel, son of Isaac Abrabanel, the Sephardic statesman, philosopher, and exegete, Benvenida Abrabanel moved to Naples with her family in 1492 after the Expulsion. Tradition has it that Benvenida became the tutor of Leonora, daughter of the Spanish Viceroy then ruling in Naples. Her charitable work was well known, and she enthusiastically supported David Reuveni in 1524/5.
>
> In 1541 the Jews were expelled from the Kingdom of Naples and the Abrabanels moved north to Ferrara, a major refuge for Sephardic Jews. Before he died in 1547, Samuel made a will naming Benvenida the general heir to his vast wealth, specifying how it should be divided among his many children. This will became a point of controversy among the Abrabanels. She expanded her financial activities and was active in helping her people until the end of her life.

general to come to Florence, including in this invitation Levantine Jews.

Florence had been devastated by political crises, plagues, and economic disasters before Cosimo came to power. He was determined to revive the economy, and felt that immigrants with skills could play an important role in his goal. Once production rose, he realized that the new goods had to be marketed, and so he searched for new trade routes, looking especially to the Ottoman Empire. But he also needed a viable port in Tuscany itself, and for this he chose the small city of Livorno, investing in land reclamation, the construction of a fortress, and the building of a fleet.

Ironically, Cosimo's attitude regarding the city of Florence itself was very different, for in 1571 he passed a law creating a ghetto. It is important to note that not all ghettos were built for the same reasons. The Venetian ghetto was an economic creation tied to, but not dictated by, Catholicism.

> **David Reuveni**
> **(d. ca. 1538)**
>
> David Reuveni was an adventurer who appeared in Venice in 1523 and convinced the Jews there that he was the brother of a King Joseph who ruled the lost tribes of Reuven, Gad, and half of Menashe in a distant land. He requested the Jews to aid him in meeting with Pope Clement VII to propose a treaty between his state and Christianity to fight the Muslims. With a letter from the pope, David Reuveni went to King John III of Portugal to request an army. His arrival aroused the Converso community there, including Diego Pires, who reverted to Judaism, taking the name Solomon Molcho. The messianic fervor Reuveni aroused continued to affect Italian Jews, but in the end he was imprisoned on charges of Judaizing.
>
> The main sources of information about him are his so-called "diary," written in Hebrew, and letters by contemporaries.

The Roman ghetto, on the other hand, was built for papal reasons and was geared toward encouraging conversion. The ghetto in Florence was built as part of Cosimo I de Medici's attempt to consolidate power. Among other things, he wanted the title of Grand Duke both for political reasons and so that he could set up a hereditary duchy. The title could only be bestowed by the pope, and so in a complex set of moves he satisfied Pius V, and the title became his in 1570. It is probable that the law creating the ghetto in 1571 was part of this. However, since no Casa dei Catechumeni, or home for converts, was established, the goal of this ghettoization could not have been conversion. If anything, the ghettoization of the Jews of Florence was a statement more of civil jurisdiction than papal control.

When the law was passed creating the ghetto, the voluntary informal community of Jews, with its small synagogues, was transformed into a regularized formal *communita* led mainly by the small elite of merchants. They gradually brought order to the space allotted to the Jews, using persuasion and fines as their main means of achieving it.

Unlike the situation in the Roman ghetto, there were no strict restrictions placed on the Jews of Florence's ghetto, and they traveled outside the ghetto selling their wares, attending fairs, and getting travel permits to go to family celebrations. The fact that the Jews continued to be members of guilds marked Florence as one of the few cities that allowed this.

Internally, the ghetto affected the Jews in a variety of ways. Ghetto life delayed marriage for some men, as they had to work longer to be able to afford setting up a home due to the dearth and hence expense of homes within the ghetto. For women the affected issue was dowry, or the symbol of status and focus of wealth for women. To protect their dowries, numerous prenuptial agreements were formulated, as they were in other ghettos. The provision of a dowry for a daughter often left a son without an inheritance. Parents tried to arrange for marriages that would get their daughters out of the ghetto to another city, which led to the diminishment of the wealth of the Florence community.

The focal point of life continued to be the family, but it was the *communita* that provided the social and economic needs of all, through the typical Jewish charities—especially for dowries and burials—by establishing a school, and supervising the *miqve*, the cemetery, and the slaughterhouse, as well as paying for the rabbi and other religious functionaries. Charity was officially voluntary, but in fact the community pressured its members into supporting it. The only choice was which charity to support. Other sources of funds were wills and fines.

Initially the small group of Levantini Jews in Florence kept a low profile and obeyed the rules of the Italian *communita*, but in 1639 they received permission to set up their own community in the same ghetto. The main difference, as it was elsewhere in Italy, was religious rite and custom. The majority of Levantini Jews, however, were more interested in living in Livorno.

When Francesco I (1574-1587) took over after Cosimo died, Livorno continued to expand. A major decision that Francesco made was to grant privileges to English merchants; this resulted in Livorno becoming England's major Mediterranean port. But Francesco's plan to invite Levantine merchants in did not materialize at this time. That only occurred when his talented and capable brother Ferdinando I (1587-1609) took over the duchy. It is he who really constructed the Livorno harbor, excavating it in record time, and building up piers, grain silos, and warehouses, as well as beautiful new housing to attract settlers. He then turned to the Levantine Jews in particular for two specific reasons: the high standard of their commercial technology, and their reputation as international traders with political influence in the Ottoman Empire. The technology included the making of special dyes and soaps, the production of fine hard hats, the recycling of waste cotton to produce a useful coarse fabric, the usage of luxury leathers, and the stringing of pearls. As for their reputation as people of influence, the Levantine Jews did try to obtain a Capitulations treaty—that is, a most-favored nation treaty—for Florence from the Ottoman sultan. Although they were unsuccessful after two years of negotiations ending in 1593, the duke at that time issued the *Livorniana*, inviting them to settle in the free port of Livorno as a foreign merchant colony.

The *Livorniana* was one of a long series of charters aimed at building up the Italian states' economic position, and was directed to all Levantine merchants. It became a prototype for Jewish settlement in other Italian cities as well. The question that has to be addressed is why the Levantine Jews would be willing to move out of the Ottoman Empire. As usual, there are push-pull forces at work. The push was that the Ottoman Empire had peaked in its power and by the end of the sixteenth century, had begun its long decline. The wealthy Levantine Jews, especially those of Sephardic origin, were aware that their important role in east-west trade was gradually being restricted, and so they looked abroad for better opportunities. The invitation to move to Livorno was a perfect match for their needs, and the needs of the Italian states.

Since the *Livorniana* was copied by other governments in Italy as well as the rest of Europe—although few if any other governments could duplicate the kind of commercial and communal success of Tuscany—it is also a primary source reflecting life at the time. It provided, first, for personal safeguards, including the right to acquire land under a twenty-five-year, automatically renewed, agreement, which ensured a sense of security. Second, religious rights were spelled out, including the right to have a synagogue, a cemetery, immunity from the Inquisition, kosher

---

***Costituzione Livorniana*, 1593**

Don Ferdinand Medici, by God's grace, third Grand Duke of Tuscany ....

To all merchants of whatever nation—Levantines, Ponentines, Spaniards, Portuguese, Greeks, Germans, and Italians, Jews, Turks, Moors, Armenians, Persians and others, I salute you.

We signify by this, our Patent Letter, that We are motivated by worthy aims, and especially by Our desire for the public good, to increase the chances for foreigners, at every opportunity, to come and bring their commerce and merchandise to Our favorite city of Pisa, and the port of Livorno, and to stay or live there with or without your families....

1. We grant to all Turkish Jews and Moors and other real merchants, free safe conduct, as well as free faculty and license, that you may come, stay, trade ... in Our city of Pisa and port of Livorno. You may also stay to trade elsewhere in all of Our ducal dominion without any obstacle or harrassment, real or personal, for the coming twenty-five years, with notice of termination required five years beforehand. However this is dependent upon the consent of the Apostolic See....

3. We desire, further, that during the said period, no inquisition, denunciation or accusation may be made against you or your families. Even though you may have lived outside of Our dominion as Christians, you may come ... and maintain yourselves in Our said city of Pisa and in Livorno, and freely trade in the other areas of Our dominion, and perform there all of your ceremonies, precepts, rites, laws and customs, according to the Jewish Law or otherwise according to your custom ... so long as it will be tolerated by the Apostolic faith as is the custom at Venice and Ferrara. We prohibit you from engaging in usury....

6. We grant you the right to deal and trade in all of the cities, territories, fairs, markets, villages and other places of Our states and to sail to the Levant, the West, Barbary, Alexandria and elsewhere under your own names or under a Christian name....

---

meat, religious books, a ban on forced conversion (especially of children), access to secular courts, no Jewish symbol worn on clothing, no enclosed and gated ghetto, and permission to both attend a university and receive a degree. Some of these religious rights had to be carefully crafted so as not to give the appearance of being anti-papal. For example, the Talmud was on the forbidden list of books, and so it was not included in the right to own religious books. The issue of the return to Judaism by Conversos is delicately evaded, by listing them as foreign "Portuguese."

A third rubric dealt with the right of the Levantine Jews to set up an organized community, dominated initially by a consul who shared power with the rabbi, but in fact ruled by a governing council of laymen called

17. We grant you the license and the right to possess printed or manuscript books of all sorts in Hebrew or other languages. However, they must be reviewed by the Inquisitor or someone else appointed for this.

18. We desire that your Jewish doctors, whether physicians or surgeons, shall be allowed to cure and medicate not only yourselves, without prejudice, but also any Christian....

19. We desire that any of you shall be allowed to study and receive degrees at our universities.

20. We grant you the right to maintain a synagogue in both the said city of Pisa and port of Livorno. You may perform all of your Jewish ceremonies, precepts, and commandments in them, and worship [according to] your rites in them and outside of them. We do not want anyone to dare to insult you in any way or commit any outrage or act of violence against you during these [religious observances] on pain of Our displeasure....

26. We forbid each of Our Christian [subjects] to dare take or accept from you any of your family, whether male or female, for the purpose of being baptized as Christians unless [that Jew] has passed the age of thirteen years....

29. We grant you all of the privileges, rights and favors which Our merchants, Florentine and Pisan citizens and Christians, enjoy. That is, you may engage in all types of crafts and in commerce of every sort. Furthermore, none of you nor your families shall be forced to wear any badge.... Furthermore, you may buy real estate.

30. Plus, we grant that each head of family can carry any sort of arms.... in all states except in Florence, Sienna, and Pistoia....

37. We grant to you the right to purchase in Pisa or in Livorno one or more pieces of land in order to be able to bury your dead in them....

42. We grant you the right to employ Christian servants and similarly Christian wet nurses.... freely quartering them in your houses in the same manner as is done in Ancona, Rome, and Bologna.

Given in Florence in Our ducal palace on the tenth of June in the year 1593 and [in the] sixth [year] of our grand-duchy of Tuscany and our other duchies.
[signed] Ferdinandus

Italian text, Schoenberg Collection, University of Pennsylvania Library.

massari, which controlled everything from appointing judges, to setting taxes, to voting on new members. Revenue came from voluntary donations, fees charged for synagogue honors, and fines for breaking rules. This Sephardic community kept out Italian and Ashkenazi Jews, the unskilled and poor, and any competitors. The next rubric was the logical extension of any organized community structure, namely judicial procedures and safeguards for the Jews. Jews were to judge internal Jewish cases, using both *halakha* for ritual issues and a kind of approximation of Jewish law, which was closer to the law of merchants, for other matters. A special impartial judge would deal with cases involving Jews and Christians.

The last rubric was that of Jewish commercial rights and privileges, the thrust of the charter from the duke's perspective. Jews could live only in Livorno and Pisa, but for trade purposes could temporarily stay anywhere in Tuscany. The duke would protect Levantine Jews and their goods from the Knights of San Stefano, who were under his control and were known for piracy on the high seas. They would also have special lower taxes, access to business loans, and regularized insurance.

The Levantine Jews, although invited to both Pisa and Livorno, generally preferred Livorno, which was cheaper, newer, and convenient in that it had no other Jewish groups. The first synagogue was built in 1602/3, and by the mid-seventeenth century the Jews made up about ten percent of the total population. Few rabbis settled in Livorno, perhaps because it was a religiously and intellectually isolated community and so was unattractive to Italian rabbis. The community was so successful that it even set up a "daughter" community in Tunis, on the southern cost of the Mediterranean, which was known as the *Gorni* in order to differentiate it from the local North African Jewish community.

The winds of change came on the heels of Martin Luther and the beginning of the Reformation in Germany. The Counter-Reformation, started by the Holy See, brought about intellectual repression and the hunting of heretics. The Inquisition was introduced in Italy in 1542, at the time that the Jesuit order was founded by Ignatius Loyola. The Jesuit order was geared toward education and proselytizing. In addition, the Index of forbidden books was created in 1564.

In 1555, Pope Paul IV (formerly Cardinal Caraffa) issued the bull *Cum nimis absurdum*, which declared in sweeping terms how the Jews were to live segregated from the Christians. There was to be only one synagogue per city, Jews were not permitted to own real estate, they could not hire Christian servants, and they were to wear some sort of badge of shame on their outer clothing. Jews were relegated to certain specific occupations, mainly buying and selling old clothes and second-hand goods; loan bankers and doctors were subject to very specific regulations. This bull introduced

***Cum Nimis Absurdum*, May 23, 1555**

As it is completely absurd and improper that the Jews, condemned by God to eternal servitude because of their guilt, should, on the pretext that they are accepted by Christian piety and permitted to live in our midst, be so ungrateful to Christians as to insult them for their mercy and presume to superiority instead of the subjection that they deserve; and because we have been informed that in Rome and elsewhere their insolence is such that they presume to live among Christians in the neighborhood of churches without distinction of dress, and even to rent houses in the more elegant streets and squares of the cities, villages, and places in which they live, to buy and possess real property, to hire Christian maids and wetnurses and other servants, and to commit other misdeeds to the shame and contempt of the Christian name; and considering that the Roman Church tolerates the Jews as evidence of the true Christian faith ... we do therefore order the following measures, which are to be perpetually valid.... (SS Paulus IV, 1555-07-14. From documentacatholicaomnia. com [Latin].)

the ghetto system into the areas under papal control. Within two months, the ghetto of Rome was completed and gradually all Jews of the Papal States had to move behind its walls, with the exception of the residents of Ancona, the papal-controlled port on the Adriatic. A small ghetto was erected there.

The city of Ancona contained Italian Jews and a smaller group of Conversos who, under protection of the previous popes, had openly returned to Judaism. In 1556, Pope Paul IV withdrew this protection and allowed the Inquisition to arrest about 100 Sephardic Jews, accusing them of heresy. A delegation rushed to Dona Gracia Nasi, now residing in Istanbul, to see if she could help. She went to see the Ottoman sultan, Sulayman the Magnificent, and convinced him to help. The sultan sent the pope a letter advising him to free all Jews who were Ottoman subjects, or he could not guarantee the safety of Christians in his empire. One third of the arrested Jews were released as a result of this letter. One third recanted their "relapse" to Judaism and were shipped out of Ancona to work in the mines (perhaps of Sardinia); their ship, however, was captured by the Ottoman navy, and the Jews were probably brought to Istanbul and freed. Twenty-three Jews who refused to admit to heresy were marched to the main piazza of Ancona and burned at the stake in an *Auto-da-fé*. When this news reached Dona Gracia, she returned to the sultan, who agreed to punish the pope by ordering a barricade of Turkish ships to be placed in the waters off the city of Ancona. This barricade remained in place for two years, at the end of which time the Italian Jews of Ancona appealed to Dona Gracia, explaining that the boycott was destroying their livelihood as well as injuring the pope's income. The boycott thus ended.

Things eased a bit for the Jews of the Papal States with the election of Pope Pius IV in 1559, but six years later, with the election of Pope Pius V, the former head of the Inquisition, all the terms of *Cum nimis absurdum* were enforced, and no Jew could live in the Papal States outside of Rome and Ancona. Some accepted the Duke of Naxos' invitation to move to Tiberius. The Duke of Naxos was also known as Don Joseph Nasi, nephew and son-in-law of Dona Gracia, who had inherited her mantle of leadership and protection of Jews.

The Roman ghetto was unique while at the same time similar in certain ways to all other ghettos. Its uniqueness was partly due to the fact that it was located in the back yard of the papacy and therefore came under the direct control of the popes, who by the mid-sixteenth century ruled an unstable Church facing a rapidly expanding Protestant Reformation. Overturning the medieval laws that declared that the Jews be treated as peaceful members of society (enacted by Pope Alexander II, 1063), and that Jews were guaranteed the benefit of the due process of law (enacted by Calixtus II, ca. 1119), the sixteenth-century papacy moved to enforce the discriminatory laws of the Fourth Lateran Council of 1215, which included the wearing of a Jewish "badge." But the papacy also changed its policy toward converting the Jews, from a relatively passive one to encouraging active attempts to do so. The burning of the Talmud, which was seen as the source of Jewish obstinacy, took place in Rome in 1553. When this did not have the desired effect, the pope moved to create a ghetto, thereby segregating the "contaminating" Jews and making it easier to batter them with an intense conversion program, which included obligatory sermons and forcible removal of those who allegedly did want to convert, and placement of them the Casa dei Catechumeni. From the popes' point of view, mass Jewish conversion would demonstrate the Catholic Church's continuing vitality.

Despite being forced into the ghetto, and despite the proselytizing activities of the Franciscans, Dominicans, and Jesuits, the Jews not only survived as Jews but even managed to achieve a measure of coexistence with their Christian neighbors, through being integrated into Rome's commercial life. Crammed into a mere seven-acre area, close to 4,000 Jews sharpened their traditional tools of survival, which they had developed over the centuries, and developed some new ones.

The initial reaction of the Jews to the creation of the ghetto was probably one of disbelief. Then their attitude probably changed to the fatalistic belief that the ghetto would be built, but that it would be temporary. Reality gradually took over, however, and decisions had to be made.

First and foremost was the question of space. How could so many people live in so small a space? The only ways to accommodate them were to subdivide apartments, make use of every available possibility, and build upwards. Pope Sixtus V allowed the ghetto to be enlarged in 1589, for his own practical purposes: the larger the Jewish population in the ghetto became, the more taxes would be collected on both the interest charged by Jewish loan bankers and Jewish businesses in general. However, overcrowding continued to be a problem, as Jews from all over the Papal states were forced to live in the ghetto of either Ancona or Rome.

A valuable primary source reflecting life in the Roman ghetto is a collection of notarial acts, a series of legal instruments written originally in Hebrew by Jewish notaries, most of whom were rabbis. The work of these notaries enabled the Jews to have almost but not quite *de facto* autonomy in settling internal affairs, using, usually, the tool of arbitration. In extreme cases, they relied on papal authorities for judicial enforcement. Disputes over space were settled this way.

Another issue concerning space had to do with rents. The Jews could not own property in the ghetto and so rented space from Gentiles, who tried to get higher rents from wealthier people. To prevent this, the Jews relied on the Jewish legal concept of *hazaqa*, or proprietary right. This established a tenant-proprietorship which secured the occupant against any kind of outbidding by his neighbor, and the community was able to enforce this through their communal control of sanctions. Living space was so valuable that it became part of wills and dowries, effectively passing these rental spaces on to the next generation. Wills were also used to prevent inheritances of any kind from going to relatives who had converted to Christianity.

Obviously some Jews did convert over the long period the Roman ghetto was in use. Some did so out of conviction, and some to escape the high walls and the overcrowding. No one really trusted these converts, which led some to become zealots, while others became disgruntled and returned to Judaism. Most lived their lives quietly, usually keeping ties with their Roman Jewish family, for there were trade and commerce connections that were not severed by the conversion. The Jews seem to have ambivalent feelings about these business ties, but they were adamant about not allowing the converts to inherit. What we do not find at all in the Roman Ghetto is issues connected to a Converso population, such as the problems of Judaizing.

Unlike the new Jewish communities north of the Papal States, the Jewish community of Rome had a long and continuous history. Stability was provided by a strong family and community structure, bound together by Judaism. The tight-knit, warm family unit was the center of daily ritual practice, and it acted as a haven within an increasingly antagonistic world. It served as the most fundamental educational tool, passing on from generation to generation the detailed laws and customs of an all-encompassing religion. The notarial acts give us glimpses of matches, marriages, divorces, and even trousseaux—the items that a bride brought into her marriage. All boys had a basic knowledge of Hebrew, and by the fifteenth century so did most girls. Many boys and girls were apprenticed to artisans to learn the crafts allowed to Jews. Girls, for example, learned the female craft of fine embroidery. Wealthier families gave their children lessons in dance and music, and rabbinic families provided intensive classes in Judaism for their sons.

The synagogue also provided stability to the Jews of Rome. Until the fifteenth century, Jewish Rome was basically Italian. Gradually the Jews from across the mountains, the so-called "ultramontani," began to arrive. The Italian Jews had at least four—and sometimes six—synagogues, while the ultramontani divided by country of origin, i.e. Provence, Germany, Sicily, Castile, and Catalonia. The arrival of the Sephardim after 1492 may have led to some friction in the beginning. *Shevet Yehuda* by Solomon ibn Verga, notes that when the Italian Jews did not want the Iberian Jews to settle in Rome, the Iberians appealed to the pope to intervene. However, this primary source is now viewed by many scholars as a literary device, and it is felt that this incident did not really happen. However, unlike in other ghettos, the need for amalgamation, combined with a long history of absorbing various groups of Jews, led to uniformity and cooperation. The "ethnic" differences had to do mainly with liturgy, custom, and languages spoken at home, resulting in the formation of separate synagogues. But the community itself, after an initial confrontation, was unified in its administration.

The formal Jewish community of Rome, or *Universita*, was composed of a sixty-man legislature or *Congrega*, divided equally between Italian Jews and non-Italian Jews. This changed in 1571, after all the Italian Jews of the Papal States were forced to move to the Roman Ghetto, giving the Italian Jews 35 of the seats. As a result of the compromise worked out by Daniel da Pisa in 1524, a council of twenty men, twelve of them Italian, ran the daily affairs of the Ghetto. The communal heads were a three-man group, called the *fattori* or *memunim*, (appointees), two of whom were Italian. The self-government was in the hands of laymen, not rabbis, who were limited to synagogue leadership. There were times that rabbis could influence issues, but that depended on their personal charisma and prestige.

There seems to have been little friction once the governing bodies were set up. Perhaps this was due to the relatively equal numbers of wealthy and middle-class people in the Italian and non-Italian groups. The best indication of cooperation and acceptance is the fact that there were many inter-communal marriages. By the second generation after the arrival of the Sephardim and Sicilians, Italian Jewish men were marrying non-Italian Jewish women.

An interesting difference in custom pertained to the financial problem involving the dowry, in the case of a wife dying during the first year of marriage. These inter-communal marriages led to practical solutions. In Tedeschi (Ashkenazi) custom, the entire dowry would be returned to the father; in Sephardic custom only half would be returned. In Italian custom, the entire dowry would remain in the hands of the husband. The Jewish notaries worked out a compromise by moving into the preliminary marriage contract of marriage (the *shtarei hittun* or *tenayim*) and setting down the details for that particular marriage. Note that the original Middle Eastern Jewish custom of *mohar*, or brideswealth, paid by the groom's family, has disappeared in favor of the Western custom of dowry, paid by the bride's family.

Marriages were arranged by parents. Cases adjudicated by the notaries indicate that children could refuse the marriages. Jewish law gave women more rights than did Christian law. Jewish women could inherit and bequeath property, they could act as their own legal agents, and they could become guardians. Their dowry was their own, and should they become widowed, they received control of it. It was outside pressure that gradually eroded these rights. Marriages were complicated by divorces, remarriages, and deaths, with details listed over who paid for what, especially in connection with children of the couple.

One thing unique to Rome was a prayer service for women (*scole delle donne*) in which a woman would lead the responses. This service was held in a room attached to the synagogue. These women could read Hebrew, and girls actually went to school, in addition to serving as apprentices. Women must also have known at least the basics of arithmetic as well as Italian, as they worked either alongside their men or independently.

By the time of the ghetto, Hebrew had become mainly a written language, used by notaries for contracts and deposition, and by scholars and intellectuals. Jews spoke Italian, which influenced their Hebrew; they also spoke Judeo-Italian, and a small group spoke an even more specific dialect, Judeo-Roman. Yet almost all of them had a reading knowledge of Hebrew, the language of the liturgy, the rituals, and the Bible.

As pragmatic and creative as the Roman Jews were, the length of time that they were enclosed in the ever more crowded ghetto, and the gradual impoverishment of the community, took its toll. At the beginning of this period, popes recognized the need for small loans and gave licenses to Jewish loan-bankers. But with the constant theoretical arguments for and against usury, and the growth not only of the Monte di Pieta but more modern banking systems, the Jewish loan-banks were superfluous by the end of the seventeenth century. Originally, too, the Romans depended on Jews for services other than running loan-banks, such as supplying things like grain and food, and producing things like tailored clothing and embroidered goods. But the popes kept restricting the ways in which Jews could work, to the point that the sale of second-hand goods became a major occupation.

Eventually life was stifling. The overcrowding delayed marriages, generating frustration and despair as intimate privacy disappeared. It fostered disease whenever the Tiber overflowed into the ghetto. After three hundred years, poverty was endemic. It took the outside force of the unified Italian State to pull down the ghetto in 1870.

With the expansion of papal rule and influence northward over the eighteenth century, one by one the dukes and rulers of the northern provinces gave in to the pressure to put "their" Jews in ghettos. In Venice, the city with the first ghetto, rules against the Jews were the most lax, possibly because of Venice's close commercial ties with the Ottoman Empire, which even sent a Jewish ambassador, Solomon Ashkenazi, to that city in the 1570s.

To add to the anti-Jewish laws, Pope Gregory XIII ordered conversionist sermons for Jews to be delivered in the synagogues on the Sabbath, usually by talented and virulent apostates. Through individual absolutions, some Jews could reopen loan-banks, but the general situation was one of repression leading to poverty. One of the worse abuses of this period was forced baptisms, especially of children. Apostate husbands demanded and received their children, and any claim on the part of any Christian that he or she had baptized a Jewish child, even if it was with water from a bucket, was recognized by the Church and the child was forcibly placed in the *Casa dei Catecumeni*. The first *Casa dei Catecumeni*, or Home for Converted Jews, was set up in Rome at the instigation of Igantius Loyola in 1543. Most of the upkeep of these Homes was imposed on the Jews themselves. Any Jew hinting at an interest in converting could be carried off, on the pretext that they should have time to "explore" their interest. Inside the Home, every endeavor would be made to convince him or her of the superiority of Christianity, and that he or she should convert. Any family member attempting to dissuade someone inside the Home could be severely punished; they could not even approach the building. This was where the so-called baptized children were brought. The attempts to convert children in this manner continued into the nineteenth century, most notoriously in the case of Edgardo Mortara in 1858 in Bologna, which will be discussed elsewhere in this volume. These actions were especially prevalent in the Papal States, and so we find Jews moving to what they considered safer places.

The Age of the Ghetto, which lasted until the start of the nineteenth century, was a decisive moment in the history of the Jews of Italy, for it affected all of them, and not just the upper classes as the Renaissance period had. According to some scholars, Jewish cultural self-awareness was defined in the space that they controlled, namely the ghetto, and this led to Jewish cultural creativity. This manifested itself in Jewish music for synagogues, decoration of *Ketubot* using Italian popular motifs, and Baroque ritual objects, to name just a few examples. And despite all of these restrictions the Jews flourished intellectually. Behind the walls of the ghetto, Jews were still open to Italian culture and wrote in Italian as well as in Hebrew. Sarah

Proposal for a Jewish College, Mantua, 1564

I, David [Rabbi David Provenzalo] have seen the distressing sight and the disturbing spectacle ... the peoples among whom we live are ever increasing in wisdom, understanding, and knowledge, and in all arts, but Israel alone is isolated, desolate, poor.... Therefore I have made up my mind ... if God be with me, to turn my house into a college for any man, for any fine young Jew.... Thus every one who seeks Jewish learning and lore may turn here....

Associated with me in this enterprise will be my oldest son [Abraham Provenzalo] ... who is a doctor of philosophy and of medicine....

II. Young students who come from out of town to board in my house will be provided with a bed, table, chair, and lamp, and will be completely free from providing for their bodily needs.... Those who come to my home shall not be transients but shall come for a period of five years....

III. Our chief study will be that which is the basis of everything: the written Torah and the oral interpretation....

IV. In studying the Bible we will read the best of the old and the new commentators....

V. We will read occasionally chapters of the best Jewish philosophers....

VI. We will fix periods for the study of Hebrew grammar....

IX. At special hours the students will learn Latin.... The students shall also write themes in Hebrew and in good Italian and Latin....

X. Those who are versed in Latin can read the scientific books dealing with logic, philosophy, and medicine.... After this he may enter practice with competent Jewish and Christian physicians....

XI ....And they will get many-sided instruction in the various forms of arithmetic, geometry, and fractions ... as well as geography....

XII. At fixed periods the students will engage in debates in our presence both in matters of Jewish law and in the sciences, in order to sharpen their minds. Each young man will learn more or less in accordance with his individual capacity—the main thing is that they be religious in spirit. Also they will gradually be taught to speak in public and to preach before congregations....

Consider this appeal, you leaders of the people. Let him who is for his people respond.... (*"Igeret me-Rabbenu David Provenzalo," Ha-Lebanon* Vol. V [1868]: 418-19, 434-35, 450-51 [Hebrew].)

Coppio Sullam is one example. The irony was that more Jews than ever were getting medical degrees, and more rabbis than ever before acquired these medical degrees. The diffusion of Jewish culture of so many varieties was due to the continued use of the printing press, as Italy became the publishing capital of the Jewish world.

~ *s* ~

While this was the situation inside Italy, an Italian Jewish community outside Italian borders was thriving. The city of Trieste, along the northern Adriatic coast, became part of the Habsburg Empire in 1382. Until the eighteenth century it was a small city of about 3,000 people; by the end of that century, it was transformed into a major commercial center, with 30,000 residents.

The small Jewish community, numbering about sixty to eighty people, was placed in a ghetto in 1697. The ghetto here consisted of thirteen houses along three streets in one of the central quarters of the city. But the ghettoization was less harsh than it was in other cities, because there were more economic opportunities and because the wealthy were permitted to live outside the ghetto walls.

When Trieste was declared a free port in 1719, the Habsburg ruler invited in people who had knowledge of commerce, including Jews. The immigration of Jews led to an expansion of the ghetto in 1753, as well as a rise in the number of rich Jews permitted to live outside its walls. These Jews were involved in finance, brokerage, and international commerce—trading in goods like grains, tobacco, sugar, cloth, and spices.

A synagogue was built in 1746; until then prayers had been held in private homes. The community became self-governing, with its rules spelled out, and this government was backed by the state. By 1800 there were four synagogues. All of the rabbis were Italian, and most of the customs followed were Italian, even though some of the Jews were of Sephardic and Ashkenazic origin. The language of the Jews, both at home and in commerce, was Italian. Rabbinic duties were defined to include making *halakhic* rulings, delivering sermons twice monthly (in Italian), teaching children and adults, officiating at weddings, tending to the sick and dying, and resolving disputes.

The eighteenth century witnessed a process of change within the free port of Trieste as the Jews obtained a firm footing there. They had no special tax on them and no distinctive signs on their person, and had the right to own real estate. The community leaders made sure to keep out non-productive Jewish immigrants, taught their children the values and work ethic of the free port—so important to the rulers—and made sure that Jewish economic law prevailed over the community. The reward was that

Jews could participate in the all-powerful *Borsa*, or Mercantile Exchange, of the city.

Emperor Joseph II passed his Edict of Toleration in 1781/2, which reinforced Jewish rights in Trieste, but also focused on the state's task, as he saw it, to transform the Jews into useful, civic-minded subjects. This task was to be accomplished via cultural transformation, using the German language and the state's system of modern education as the tools. Jews all over the empire were ordered to take surnames and German first names. The Jews in Trieste already had Italian or Sephardic surnames, so they were at an advantage over most of the other Jews. All documents had to be in German, so the Jews of Trieste translated their documents from Italian, but they continued to keep their original records in Italian.

Attendance at state-supervised schools were made compulsory for boys aged five to fifteen, but Jewish education was in place long before this law, although it was usually conducted by individual teachers. The heavy Italian-Jewish curriculum was supplemented by secular classes in geography, history, and German as a second language. New methods were used within a Jewish framework, and only in Trieste were the secular and Jewish curricula taught in one building, known as the *Scuola Pia Normale sive Talmud Tora* (Religious-normal school or Talmud Torah). It opened in 1782, and was paid for by the Jewish community.

The community, led by the rabbi, enthusiastically accepted this new curriculum and adapted it to their needs. For example, morality was taught using Jewish texts such as *Pirkei Avot* (*Ethics of our Fathers*). There were no provisions for the education of girls, so the Jews continued to educate them with private teachers. Jewish women had long been teachers of the youngest children. Jews could go to the university, and could practice law, and certainly medicine, in Trieste.

This warm response was due, in part, to the acculturation of the Italian Jews, who had no fear of secular studies. The wealthiest groups saw this modern education as a way to promote ever-further integration with non-Jews. They saw proof of this in the abolition of the ghetto in 1785.

The only two laws of the Habsburg monarchy that gave the Trieste Jews pause were those creating civil marriages, with all of the details spelled out, and the law of 1788, which conscripted Jews into the army. In the entire Habsburg Empire, only the Jews of the Italian-speaking cities thought that civic and religious duties could be reconciled, and that the government could be asked to accommodate the needs of Jewish soldiers; the Jews of the rest of the empire feared conscription as a threat to Judaism. However, no Trieste sons actually were conscripted, because the government felt that they served the state better by working in commerce.

As for marriage laws, there were two cases that rocked the Jewish community, resulting in a civil-religious mix. It was the Jewish community, however, that prevailed in the end, because it still had the power to pressure its members.

Trieste was conquered by Napoleon, but it went back to Austria-Hungary after his defeat in 1814. Some Jews played an active part in the Italian *Risorgimento*, identifying themselves as Italian. Others participated in the Irredentist struggle, which culminated in Trieste's return to Italian control in 1919.

Many scholars feel that as Papal power expanded and Catholic reaction took over in Italy, with the shadow of the Inquisition putting a pall on creativity, the only sparks of cultural innovation were to be found in the ghetto. Within these walls, Jews were an isolated microcosm, continuing to produce intellectual works as though the Renaissance had never ended.

It is within this context that we must understand Rabbi Moses Hayyim Luzzatto (known by the acronym Ramchal). Born in Padua in 1707, he received an excellent Jewish and general education. His Hebrew was magnificent, and he wrote both poetry and dramas. But that was only one facet of his creativity. He also wrote a book of ethics, *Mesilat Yesharim*, which became one of the most popular books of the *Mitnagdim,* the eastern European Jews opposed to Hasidism, in their *yeshivot* in Eastern Europe. A third facet of his creativity got him into trouble: claiming that he heard a divine voice, or *magid*, he recorded his revelations. He was eventually accused of Sabbateanism and was pressured into not writing Kabbala anymore. He could not deal with this ban and left Italy, first for Amsterdam and then for Israel, where he died in 1747, before his fortieth birthday. In a sense Luzzatto represents the split personalities of the Italian Jewish scholar, for his Hebrew poetry and dramas were admired by the Haskala writers of the modern period, his ethical works are still studied in Lithuanian *yeshivot*, and his Kabbalistic material is studied by Hasidim.

Recommended Reading

Bonfil, Roberto. *Jewish Life in Renaissance Italy.* Los Angeles: University of California Press, 1994.

Davis, Robert C., and Benjamin Ravid, eds. *The Jews of Early Modern Venice.* Baltimore: Johns Hopkins University Press, 2001.

Dubin, Lois. *The Port Jews of Habsburg Trieste: Absolutist Politics and Enlightenment Culture.* Stanford: Stanford University Press, 1999.

Myers, David N., et al, eds. *Acculturation and Its Discontents.* Toronto: University of Toronto Press, 2008.

Siegmund, Stefanie B. *The Medici State and the Ghetto of Florence: The Construction of an Early Modern Jewish Community.* Stanford: Stanford University Press, 2006.

Stow, Kenneth. *Jewish Life in Early Modern Rome: Challenge, Conversion, and Private Life.* Great Britain: Ashgate Publishing, 2007.

Costituzione Livorniana, 1593

Chapter 6

THE WINDS OF CHANGE

The French Revolution of 1789 and the ensuing invasion of Italy by French forces brought with them new ideas of equality and democracy. The French troops quickly did away with the civil limitations of Jews in 1796, and physically threw down the walls of the various ghettos. But when the French withdrew in 1798, the reaction against all of their new ideas was strong. Equality for the Jews was no exception. In many cities Jews were attacked, houses were sacked, and ghettos were recreated. Napoleon returned in 1800 and set up "sister republics," which promoted toleration, in the north. Jews entered regular civic life, even joining the army. Because the French had confiscated church property, there was suddenly an opportunity to buy land, an action that had been forbidden to the Jews earlier. Most Jews were poor, but each community had a small number of people who had liquid capital and were ready to invest. With barriers falling, Jews could also enter any profession. In his attempt to modernize, emancipate, and unify the Jews, Napoleon called for the creation of a "Sanhedrin" (a kind of Jewish Parliament) in Paris in 1806, using a Jewish term from the era when Israel was independent. The Jews of Italy sent 29 delegates to the call for a "Sanhedrin" in Paris, and Rabbis Salvatore Benedetto Segre (1757-1809) of Vercelli and Abraham Cologna (1755-1832) of Mantua became vice presidents of the rabbinical assembly, assuming positions elected by the members of the "Sanhedrin." They set up *Consistoires*, which controlled the religious schools, among other things, and even ensured that patriotism be taught.

With the fall of Napoleon in 1814 the Congress of Vienna, headed by Count Metternich, tried to turn back the clock and return to the absolute rule of kings and to old institutions and ideas. However, once freedom is tasted it is impossible to destroy, and although the ghetto walls of Italy were rebuilt, the internal life of the Jews had already been transformed.

On an economic level, King Victor Emanuel I of the House of Savoy was aware of the prominent role that the Jews played in Piedmont. Therefore,

Timeline

GENERAL		JEWISH
French Revolution	1789	Ghetto walls thrown down
Napoleon invades Italy	1800	
Congress of Vienna	1814	Return to ghetto
Edict of King Victor Emanuel I	1829	Collegio Rabbinico in Padua
Revolution – unsuccessful	1831	
Revolution – Constitutional monarchy	1848	
	1858	The Mortara Affair
Kingdom of Italy	1861	
	1800—1865	Lifetime of SHADAL
	1862	"Il Corriere Israelitico", in Trieste Equality for Jews
Completion of unification of Republic of Italy	1870 1882	Dedication of Temple of Florence
	1897	First Zionist Congress, Basel
Jewish mayor of Rome	1907	
Jewish Prime Minister	1909	
Invasion of Libya	1911	
	1858—1922	R. Margulies
	1883—1951	R. Umberto Cassuto
Balkan War – Rhodes	1912	
World War I	1914—1918	
National Fascist Party	1919	
	1920	Consortium of Italian Jewish Communities
Mussolini as Prime Minister	1922	
	1926	Mussolini meets with Chaim Weizmann
Hitler becomes Chancellor	1930/1 1933	Union of Italian Jewish Communities
Invasion of Ethiopia	1935	

when he passed the edict of January 1814 which was aimed at restoring life to pre-Napoleonic times, he was open to special requests made by the Jews, who hoped to avoid being forced back into the ghettos. He did not insist on the Jews' attaching degrading yellow symbols on their outer clothing, he allowed them to work in any trade, and he gave them five years to sell their newly-acquired real estate. In many cases the king did not enforce the sale of that real estate. However, the Jews did have to return to the ghettos.

The next few decades witnessed economic disasters in Piedmont as a result of drought and failed crops, lack of investment capital and a credit system, and backward laws governing commerce. There was growing unemployment and poverty. Even the silk industry, which employed about 75,000 workers, was in crisis. In addition to these factors, the king was pressured by the Republic of Genoa, which had been transferred to the House of Savoy by the Congress of Vienna, to allow Jews to invest in Piedmontese ports. The Republic included the port cities of Genoa, Savona, and Nice, all of which wanted to attract Jews to develop their port as they had developed Livorno, to the south of Genoa.

Due to all of these economic reasons, plus the perception—accurate or not—of Jewish wealth, the king did not force the Jews of his domain to divest themselves of land holdings or any other property outside the ghetto walls. Thus the Jews not only helped to develop maritime trade and build up the harbors, but they also invested in the textile industry and in agriculture; they even bought some *latifundia* estates from land-rich but cash-poor nobles to break the property down for resale to small farmers.

To achieve this, the Jews negotiated directly with King Victor Emanuel, and not with the aristocracy, which continued to view the Jews negatively. The positive economic activity helped Jews create allies among intellectuals, high government officials, and even the military. What made this work, too, was the political environment in Piedmont.

Secret political societies of liberals were formed, and the ideals of liberty included the recognition of the Jews as equals. This period, known as the *Risorgimento* or Reawakening, was not very successful at the beginning. The *Carbonari*, or workers for Italian freedom, staged an unsuccessful revolution in 1831. It was after that fiasco that a real leader appeared, in the person of Giuseppe Mazzini, who came to be known as the "prophet" of the *Risorgimento*. He led the newly-formed political organization *Giovane Italia*, and was joined by Giuseppe Garibaldi, a military leader of note. They were involved in the Revolution of 1848, which presented a constitution to set up a constitutional monarchy. They chose Carlo Alberto, King of Sardinia, to be king, and he took the lead in the liberal movement, providing the stability needed for success. The final personality to join these three was Count Camillo Cavour, who became the brains behind the reunification of Italy.

As a result of the failure of the Revolution of 1848, Carlo Albert stepped down. His son Victor Emanuel II continued liberalism and adopted the constitution for his kingdom, which now included Savoy. The House of Savoy had transformed itself from an autocratic, Catholic, aristocratic entity into one that was liberal, democratic, and secular. As each Italian province voted to join Sardinia, it too adopted the constitution. In 1850, Cavour became prime minister, and his secretary was Isacco Artom, one of the leading Jewish personalities of Piedmont. Middle-class Piedmontese Jews were a significant political force because so many of them fit the Piedmontese electoral law that required literacy, owning property, and having a profession. They had worked to have Cavour elected. They also joined the voluntary militias and the Piedmontese army, which were two major forces in unifying Italy. The majority of poorer Jews followed the traditional Jewish leaders, who were skeptical of the new political world. This changed only gradually.

In 1859 Lombardy joined the kingdom, and in 1860 Garibaldi and his 1,000 men marched southward, forcing the Kingdom of the Two Sicilies to join as well. By 1861 the Kingdom of Italy was declared under the house of Savoy, and the Jews were emancipated everywhere except in the Papal States and those territories under Austrian control. By 1870, Rome was also invaded by the Italians and forced to join; Italy's unification was almost complete. It was symbolic that the troops entering Rome were led, in part, by a Jewish officer named Mortara, brother of Monsignor Mortara, who had been kidnapped as a boy and converted to Christianity. It was also symbolic that the "breach of Porta Pia," in front of the ghetto, was led by a Jewish captain named Segre. Immediately after Rome became part of the state, in October 1870, the king ordered that "all unequal treatment among citizens in Rome and in the Roman provinces" would cease.

Jews were now integrated successfully in Italian society. There are various elements that went into this success, including the fact that emancipation occurred at the same time as unification and independence,

The Mortara Affair (1858)

Six-year-old Edgardo Mortara was kidnapped by the papal police in 1858 and taken from Bologna to the *Casa dei Catechumeni* in Rome. The Catholic conversionists responsible for this were acting on the testimony of a Catholic servant girl, who stated that five years earlier she had secretly baptized the child while he was sick. The parents tried in vain to get the child back, but the church maintained that the baptism was valid and that no Christian child could be raised by Jewish parents.

The case of Edgardo Mortara became an international *cause célèbre*. In Italy the Kingdom of Sardinia, which was leading Italian unification, used the case to reinforce its claim that the Papal States were ruled by medieval minds whose philosophies were still rooted in anti-Semitism. Jewish organizations and prominent personalities in Italy, the United States, France, Britain, Austria, and Germany reacted, as did the governments of these countries. But Pope Pius IX refused to give in.

The Mortara case solidified the general world opinion that the rule of the Pope was an anachronism, and by 1870 his temporal power collapsed with the completion of the unification of Italy.

Edgardo Mortara chose to remain a Catholic and spent a good part of his life preaching to the Jews to convert. He died in Belgium in 1940, a month before the Nazi invasion, thereby escaping possible arrest as a Jew.

that there was no linguistic barrier, and that the number of Jews was relatively small. Being "Italian," with a common national consciousness, was something new, and the Jews were part of this "nation" from its beginning. As they lost their earlier "corporate" or separate medieval state, some say that they became simply Italian individuals with a specific religious and ethnic identity. It was an easy jump for Jews to leave the restrictive ghetto system and the poverty that accompanied both the constrictions and the taxes imposed on them and move into the middle class. Most Jews were literate both in Hebrew and in the Italian dialect of their particular city, qualities that placed them above the majority of the Italian population. It has been said that anti-Semitism was weak at this time, yet it prevailed in a different form—that of perpetuating generic and literary stereotypes of the Jews. Here and there, there were some medieval-style pogroms and allegations.

Scholars explain that there was little need to reform Judaism itself because over the centuries, despite some traumatic confrontations and polarizing incidents, Italian Jews had learned that they had to coexist with other Jews despite differences of customs, and so were already aware of the benefits of religious pluralism.

Rabbis did not feel a need to "reform" Judaism, as some did in Germany, but rather, as guardians of tradition, saw nonobservant Jews as sinners rather than schismatics, and welcomed them to the synagogue when they came for family rites of passage. Italian rabbis formed links with the other European rabbis and intellectuals, and were aware of the Haskala movement as well as the Reform movement in Germany. Neither movement made any impression on Italian Jews, who retained their particular attitude to Judaism. However, there were conversions, as some patriotic Jews made the serious cultural decision that being a Jew was an obstacle to the new unified national state. Others converted in order to marry non-Jews, and this number grew as the years passed.

In the period between the formation of the republic and the First World War, Italian Jews were integrated into general society: they became psychologically and intellectually Italian. The year 1870 marked the end of the Piedmontese phase of Italian nationalism and the beginning of what has been described as the collective Italian consciousness of unity. Ironically, this unity diminished the role of the Jews, for this more romantic form of nationalism played on themes of shared origins, history, and religion, all of which automatically excluded Jews. Yet at this same point in time, Jews became more and more involved in politics, public life, the army, the university, and the press.

In the encounter between the Jewish and Italian cultures, it was inevitable that the Jewish one would succumb to the Italian one. Jews moved out of small communities into larger ones, and as a result the strict observance of the details of Judaism declined. The number of Jews remained the same, at about 40,000, but the Jewish percentage of the Italian population dropped from .25% to .1%. This was due in large part to the drop in the Jewish birth rate and to the growing number of intermarriages.

There was broad participation of Jews in national life. In politics, there was a Jewish mayor of Rome—Ernesto Nathan—from 1907 to 1913 and Jewish members of the senate and cabinet, and a Jewish man named Luigi Luzzatti became prime minister in 1909. In the arts, Italo Svevo and Alberto Moravia were famous Jewish authors, and Amadeo Modigliani was an Italian-Jewish painter and sculptor. Jews made up 8% of university professors, and they joined the army officer corps. All ghetto characteristics disappeared. The ghetto trades of working in second-hand goods evolved into becoming involved in antiques, retail trade, and textile manufacturing.

Ernesto Nathan (1848-1921)

Ernesto Nathan, born in England, visited Italy during his youth. He met Giuseppe Mazzini there, and was attracted by his radical political views. After Italy was unified in 1870, he moved to Rome to become the manager of Mazzini's newspaper *Roma del Popolo*. He was a republican and an advocate of a secular state. He became an Italian citizen in 1888, and the following year was elected to the City Council of Rome. He was elected mayor of Rome in 1907, the first Jew to hold this office, and was re-elected in 1911, holding office until 1913. As mayor, he worked to control the city's building programs and to promote secular education programs, opening over 150 kindergartens. He was also involved in constructing public works, a public transport system, and a city energy company, and restoring archaeological works. He enlisted in the army in 1915, and, although over 70 by that time, served at the front as a lieutenant.

By the second half of the nineteenth century, the preponderance of the Jews were state functionaries.

Despite this participation in secular life, there was also a revival of Jewish culture. At its center was a Collegio Rabbinico, which started in Padua in 1829 and is considered to be the first modern rabbinical seminary. It moved from there to Rome, and was led by Rabbi Samuel David Luzzatto, known as SHADAL. Luzzatto (1800-1865) was a well known Bible scholar who translated the Bible and wrote a commentary on the Pentateuch and some of the Prophets. He also re-translated the prayer book, or Siddur, making it more accessible. His vast knowledge of modern and traditional studies as well as his mastery of Hebrew added to his luster.

Samuel David Luzzatto, SHADAL (1800-1865)

A scholar, poet, Bible commentator and philosopher, Samuel David Luzzatto was an outstanding nineteenth-century intellectual leader of Italy. Born in Trieste and educated there, in 1829 he was appointed professor of the newly established rabbinical college of Padua, and there he spent the rest of his life.

Luzzatto's versatility and erudition are seen in his letters as well as in his scholarly works, which were written mainly in Hebrew and Italian. His Hebrew commentary on the Pentateuch and other books of the Bible reveal his critical thinking as well as his attitude to Judaism and philosophy. He developed his own positive system of religious philosophy, while opposing Greek philosophy. He also embraced a form of religious Zionism, setting the groundwork of Zionism in Italy. His translation of the Italian rite prayer is still used today.

The debates over the disintegration of Jewish culture and identity are reflected in Jewish newspapers like *Il Vessillo Israelitico*, which was the longest running such publication. It was founded by Giusseppe Levi in Vercelli in 1853, and edited by him until his death in 1874, when it came under the editorship of Rabbi Flaminio Servi of Casale until it closed in 1922. It reflected the attitudes of affluent bourgeois Jews, and covered topics like the organization of the Jewish communities, which was a source of contention since non-observant and even intermarried Jews were forced to pay taxes to the community. Mixed marriages were debated, as was the decadence of Jewish culture, the lack of attachment to tradition, and Zionism. The paper avoided Italian politics, was faithful to the government, and reflected a strong provincialism. In contrast to this was the outlook expressed in *Il Corriere Israelitico*, which was founded in 1862 in Trieste. From 1896 it was under the editorial hand of the intellectual Dante Lattes until it closed in 1914, only to reopen as *Israel* in 1916. This publication was guided by the new Italian Jewish elite of rabbis such as Margulies, Artom, Cassuto, and Lattes, and stressed Italian-Jewish unity, the strengths of Judaism, and Zionism. The role of this publication became extremely important after the Racial Laws of 1938 were passed.

Unlike most rabbis in the rest of Europe, the Italian rabbis themselves supported the *Haskala*, or Enlightenment. The Rabbinical College educated these rabbis in traditional Jewish lore, but combined these teachings with the ideas of cultural renewal. For example, SHADAL emphasized the loyalty of Jews to the land of their birth or residence. In other words, one could love Italy without giving up one's Jewish identity and connection to the land of Israel. The rabbis as a group backed the *Risorgimento* and helped establish the main instrument of modernization and acculturation: the

Elia [Elijah] Benamozegh (1822-1900)

Born in Livorno to wealthy Moroccan parents, Elia Benamozegh was appointed rabbi of Livorno, where he also taught in the rabbinical school. His scholarly works, written in Hebrew, Italian, and French, centered on showing the connections between Judaism and contemporary secular philosophy. His Judaism— unlike SHADAL's—focused on the essential roles of Kabbala, defending it against attacks. He saw Judaism as a synthesis of universal eternal truths found in all religions and philosophies, demonstrating this in one of his most famous works, *Israel et l'Humanite*.

Front of synagogue of Florence,
nineteenth century, Moorish style
(Photograph, E. Fodde-Reguer collection)

Jewish schools. SHADAL was not alone in his activities: Rabbi Lelio Della Torre (1805-71) and Rabbi Elia Benamozegh (1822-1900) were equally involved.

Yet at the end of the nineteenth century, Jewish life was still traditional and very family-oriented, with the continued observance of life cycle rites and major holidays. Religion became more private, but the changes to Judaism were not intended to reform it, as German Jews were reforming their religion, but merely to modernize external aspects of worship. However, there was a decline in the number of functioning synagogues, from 108 in 67 communities across Italy to 38, located in only the very large cities. This is part of what led to the construction of the huge synagogues, or *Tempio*, that were built in Turin, Florence, Milan, Rome, and Trieste.

In the nineteenth century, Jews renamed their place of worship *Tempio*, which reflects its change from place of study, congregation, and prayer to place of prayer and socializing. The intimate synagogues of the ghetto were deemed inadequate to express the new rights, centralizing tendencies, and wealth of the Jews, and so a series of elaborate structures was planned, demonstrating the Jews' new identification with the new Italy.

The architecture that Jews built all over the world reflects their status and their relationship with the countries in which they were living. From the choices they made one can extract a strongly expressed ideological statement. The synagogues that were built in the late nineteenth century in Italy reflect the struggle of the Jewish communities with their new independence and equal status. These buildings are the visual expression of a group of people trying to establish their distinctiveness within Italy, but at the same time solidarity with Italy and Italians. They also reflect shifts within Jewish communal life, as well as the priorities established by the Jewish religion.

There are certain standard elements that all synagogues have: they are oriented such that the community prays facing Jerusalem, and the holy ark is situated to inform the congregation of this direction. The position of the *bimah* (usually the place from which the cantor leads prayers) shifted with time; in some communities it is very close to the ark, but in others it is more centrally located. The women's section is usually in a balcony area. Most synagogues are brightly lit open spaces.

The Jews were free to build whatever kind of building they wanted, and at this time they had enough money to do so. However, because they lacked an artistic tradition, they had to turn to non-Jewish architects and non-Jewish architectural forms. Three of the main nineteenth-century synagogues are in Rome, Milan, and Florence. All three have different architectural styles, which indicates a diversity of expression. The forms that they used differed from church architecture, because they did not want to use the same forms of expression as the people that had oppressed them for so long. They also wanted to show their individuality. The Jews of Florence chose the popular "Moorish" style, which used formal elements from mosques, as the style associated the Jews with their origins in the Middle East. Because this style was practically unseen in Italy, this was a good way to distinguish the synagogue from the church.

The Jews of Florence wanted to express their appreciation for their equal status and emancipation. They also had a strong city pride and wanted to make a building that would beautify it. Work began in 1874, and the synagogue was dedicated in 1882. The plot of land on which it stands was then on the outskirts of the city, and the synagogue itself is placed back from the street, with a courtyard filled with plants from Israel, making even the smell of the space distinct from the rest of the city. The domes are Moorish in style, as are the geometric and floral decorations. The synagogue's main space is open and light-filled, marking a distinction from churches, which focus on creating mysterious space through the use of dramatic shadows, columns, and niches.

The synagogue in Rome is quite different. Its style is more eclectic, and it is not part of a street setting, but was constructed on an open area next to the ghetto, surrounded by a gate. It is spacious inside, and on the sides of the main ark are two arks from ghetto synagogues, as though the architects were determined to incorporate the older elements into the newer ones, to stress the difference in size and their different statuses. The decorations are lavish, but also eclectic.

The synagogue in Milan is the most conservative of the three. Only the façade remains of the original building, as it was bombed during World War II. The façade is simple, and the synagogue is not trying to draw attention to itself. It is purely functional, reflecting the attitude of this community.

Other cities with large nineteenth-century synagogues include Livorno, Turin, and Trieste. It is ironic that so much effort and money was put into these buildings at just the time that the Jewish communities themselves were beginning to shrink through acculturation and intermarriage.

After SHADAL's death in 1865, traditional studies once again declined, but they were saved by Hirsch Perez Chajes (1876-1927), and by Rabbi Samuel Hirsch Margulies (1858-1922), who moved to Florence in 1899 when the Collegio Rabbinico moved there as well. He attracted a cadre of students, and together they worked to revive Jewish studies. The Pro Cultura movement was started, with the goal of linking traditional Jewish studies with scientific methods. A weekly newspaper, *La Settimana Israelitica*, was printed, and in it he and his students addressed the problems of Italian Jews. Margulies also favored political Zionism as a tool for recovering Judaism, and renewal of Jewish identity through Modern Hebrew. His mantle was inherited by Umberto Cassuto (1883-1951), the historian, rabbi, and Bible scholar.

Samuel Hirsch Margulies (1858-1922)

Born and raised in Eastern Europe, Samuel Hirsch Margulies was educated in the Breslau Jewish Theological Seminary as well as at the German universities of Breslau and Leipzig. After serving as a rabbi in Germany from 1885 to 1890, he was appointed chief rabbi of Florence. When the Collegio Rabbinico Italiano was transferred to Florence from Rome, he became its head. His position there enabled him to educate and train many of Italy's spiritual leaders, bringing about a spiritual renaissance. He was also active in reviving traditional Jewish life in Italy, in part by founding and editing a learned journal published by the Collegio, *Revista Israelitica*. On a more popular level, he was an initiator of the weekly *"Settimane Israelitica."*

Umberto (Moshe David) Cassuto
(1883-1951)

Educated simultaneously in the University of Florence and the Collegio Rabbinico Italiano in his native city, Umberto Cassuto combined Jewish traditional education with secular studies. Rabbi Samuel Hirsch Margulies had a profound influence on him, and after ordination Cassuto taught at the Collegio Rabbinico and served as assistant rabbi of Florence. His outstanding scholarship, mainly on the history of the Jews of Italy, brought him international recognition. When Margulies died in 1922, Cassuto was appointed his successor as both rabbi of Florence and director of the Collegio Rabbinico. After three years, however, Cassuto resigned to become professor of Hebrew language and literature at the University of Florence, where he concentrated on Bible studies. In 1933 he moved to the University of Rome, and while living there also catalogued the Hebrew manuscripts of the Vatican Library.

After the 1938 Racial Laws were passed, Cassuto, a long-time Zionist, accepted an invitation to become the chair of Bible studies at Hebrew University, moving to Jerusalem in 1939. There he published numerous works on biblical research, including traditional-style commentaries. He was also editor-in-chief of the *Biblical Encyclopedia*, actively involved in preparing the first volumes.

One of Umberto Cassuto's sons, Nathan, was also a rabbi in Florence, but was killed by the Nazis. Another son, David, became an architect in Israel, playing a key role in rebuilding Jerusalem's Jewish Quarter.

~ ❧ ~

Between the time of the unification of Italy and the First World War, the major economic problems in the north eased with industrialization. This was not the case in the south, where emigration was so heavy that between 1880 and 1914 600,000 Italians left for places like North and South America.

In 1882, Italy joined with Germany and Austria-Hungary to form the Triple Alliance. Italy, one of the last major European countries to unify, had joined the grab for colonies late, and was interested in the Balkans, especially Albania. In 1911, Italy invaded Libya, staking a claim to part of North Africa.

When World War I started in 1914, Italy did not join in the fighting but remained neutral, secretly negotiating with the Allies. In the Treaty of London, April 26, 1915, Italy switched sides in return for a promise to receive Trieste, Gorizia, Fiume and northern Dalmatia. The next month,

Italy attacked Austria. The war was harsh, and Italy lost millions of soldiers as well as civilians. Jews signed up to fight in the war, demonstrating Jewish patriotism for their country. They served wherever Italy fought, and many were decorated for valor. At the end of the fighting, Italy did not get all that was promised in the Treaty of London, and this left a sore spot in the post-war mindset which, in part, led to the rise of Fascism.

Post-war Italy was in ferment, with no stable government. The deep economic crisis brought inflation as well as a rise in the cost of living. As a result, there were riots in 1919, peasants occupied fields, and workers and trade unions went on strike in the industrialized north. The 1919 election was the first one for which there was universal suffrage, but it was chaotic, for too many small parties were involved. The failure of this election led to internal tension and high taxes. The Socialist and Communist parties terrified the middle class and alienated millions of veterans by refusing to allow them to join their parties. The final element adding to the ferment was the Versailles Treaty, June 28, 1919, which gave Trieste, Trento, and Trentino to Italy, but not Fiume and Dalmatia, as had been promised by the Allies.

The National Fascist Party was formed in March 1919, and was led by Benito Mussolini. At first the party combined pragmatism, revolutionary trade unionism, nationalism, and imperialism. It played off of discontent, the ineffective parliament, and the reactionary groups of the ruling class. During the massive country - wide strike which started in July 1922, Mussolini led a so-called "March on Rome," (which in fact involved a train ride), and the king decided to give him the mandate to form a new government in October. Fascism was thus not imposed on Italy, but was widely popular, especially in the rising lower-middle-class, the young, and among many intellectuals.

Mussolini's first government included both liberal and populist ministers, for he was a shrewd politician, and he was quick to set up his own armed force, called the Voluntary Militia for National Security, in 1923. Violence quickly became a signature mark of the Fascists, as millions of veterans joined the party. Its strongest opponent was the Socialist party. Between 1920 and 1922, as many as 600 anti-fascists—usually socialist workers—were killed in street fighting. Mussolini reformed the method of voting by making the country into one single national constituency, and with the assassination of some of his opponents, and the weakness of a king who could not defy him, by 1925 Mussolini had set up a dictatorship. By 1929 he was in control of the press, the radio, the schools, and the economy. To get a job, one had to be a member of the Fascist Party. Mussolini completed his total control by signing the Lateran Treaty with the Vatican, which traded off a newly created state of Vatican City and Catholic control of the schools for papal backing.

Jews also joined the Fascist Party, as patriotism evolved into a kind of secular religion. By 1938 it had over 10,000 Jewish members, despite Mussolini's friendship with the newly elected Chancellor of Germany, Adolph Hitler.

It is not easy to define Mussolini's position toward the Jews and Judaism when he first came to power. As early as 1922 he declared that he respected all religions, but only Catholicism was the religion of the state. He was not a racist, in part because of the high degree of assimilation of Italian Jews, and he had some Jewish friends, especially Margherita Sarfatti, the art critic and his eventual biographer. She was the editor of the art and literature section of Mussolini's *Popolo d'Italia*, and co-editor of *Gerarchia*, the Fascist Party's monthly ideological review. She ran an intellectual salon for important Fascists for many years. She was also Mussolini's mistress, until she was exiled just before the war began. However, some scholars say that Mussolini was an anti-Semite, but his pragmatism and unsystematic character kept him from developing an anti-Semitic program at first.

Mussolini used Jews and Jewish Zionists to further his expansionist foreign policy, hoping that he could thereby weaken the British in the eastern Mediterranean. In 1926, he therefore met with Dr. Chaim Weizmann, president of the World Zionist Organization. Their meeting was a cordial one, as was his meeting in 1927 with Rabbi David Prato, who was about to leave Italy to take the position of grand rabbi in Alexandria, Egypt. Mussolini was intent on keeping a connection with all Italian Jews living in the Muslim world, whether in Tunisia, then under French control, in Egypt, then under British control, or in Libya, which was then under Italian control.

Mussolini's interest in using international Zionism against the British in Palestine led him to agree to meet with members of the Zionist Executive Committee, first with Dr. Victor Jacobson, in June 1927, and later that year with Nahum Sokolov. He even created an Italy-Palestine Committee. But it should be noted that while he praised "international Zionism" within this context, he was only too quick to turn against it when Italian Jews became Zionists, accusing them of dual loyalty.

Internally, Mussolini's restructuring of the state also standardized the Italian Jewish communities by obliging them to join a central representative body. The groundwork had been laid by the Royal Decree of 1920, which had created a Consortium of Italian Jewish Communities to oversee everything of general interest to Judaism and Jews. The Consortium tried to stay out of politics in the early 1920s, praising all pro-Jewish actions of the government and encouraging all Jews to act as "good Italians." It reclaimed Jewish values and traditions such as the Hebrew language, but there were internal fights over identity, and disagreements between rabbis and laymen over a multitude of issues, not only religious ones. An additional problem was an economic one: how would the Consortium pay for all of its activities.

The Consortium was responsible for, among other things, helping to establish new communities in the Italian colonies, like Libya. In 1930, another royal decree turned the Consortium into the Union of Italian-Jewish Communities, established mandatory contributions from member communities, oversaw elections of leaders, defined the role of rabbis, and answered to the state. The chief rabbi of Rome became the chief rabbi of Italy. The Union's goals were spelled out in detail, declaring that it was also to represent Jewish communities abroad. Its members included all Jews; any Jew refusing to be included had to leave Judaism. The imposed contributions were based on the incomes and budgets of the communities. The elections of both lay leaders and rabbis were clearly required, and the latter was to be responsible only for spiritual direction. The nominations of the rabbis were to be approved by the Minister of the Interior. This 1930 royal decree was modified in 1931, specifically naming twenty-six "communities," with the small ones, like Siena, attached to larger ones, like Florence. The Jewish communities were now a state organization, centralized and authoritarian, but they had the right to exist, and most Italian Jews favored this law. Nonetheless, the request of the Union that secular schools and universities avoid scheduling classes and on the Sabbath was ignored.

Frustrated with being given only the city of Fiume in 1924, Mussolini planned to expand into the Mediterranean, the Balkans, and Africa. He had already intervened in the Italian economy by controlling the electrical power companies and the chemical and metallurgical industries. After the crash of 1929, he expanded state intervention into other industries and into banking, and by the late 1930s the state controlled a majority share in most companies. It was only a matter of time before he would make a move, and he did so in October 1935 by attacking Ethiopia. This step was denounced by the free world, especially Britain, and Mussolini retaliated by starting a propaganda war against the British in both Egypt and Palestine. This contributed to Arab unrest and the Arab Revolt of 1936 in Palestine.

For the Jews of Italy, the conquest of Ethiopia was seen as a national event as well as a Jewish one. They already knew of the existence of Jewish groups in northern Ethiopia who were known locally as *falashas*. The Union of Jewish Communities was placed in charge of assisting Ethiopian Jews, and two Communities—one in Addis Ababa and one in Dire Dawa—were organized. Tangible contact was thus made between Italian and Ethiopian Jews.

Libyan Jews, too, now came directly under the control of the centralized system of Fascist Italy. Over the years since Italy had taken over Libya, the Jewish community there had divided into a modernizing group—usually those economically better off—and a traditional group. Italian bureaucrats sent overseas were accustomed to the usually more modern Italian Jews, and did not know what to make of the more traditional Libyan Jews, who refused to send their children to school on Saturdays, for example. At first their observances were permitted, but then in 1932-1933 Saturday school attendance was made mandatory, which resulted in the dismissals of some Jewish students. The Union of Jewish Communities became involved, and Rabbi Gustavo Castelbolognesi of Padua, was sent to deal with this issue, as well as to create a unified Jewish community with a new chief rabbi of Libya.

This event directly preceded the appointment of Italo Balbo as governor of Libya, in 1934. The many problems concerning Libyan Jews frustrated the new governor, who was like the other Italian bureaucrats accustomed to the more westernized and sophisticated Italian Jews. He not only refused to budge on the mandatory Saturday classes, but expanded the law in December, requiring Jews to keep their shops open on Saturdays. The final conflict took place in 1935. The crux of the matter was a forced marriage between a thirty-five-year-old Jewish man and a fifteen-year-old girl, each of a high social position. Balbo clashed with Rabbi Castelbolognesi, who backed the marriage, and their official discord became personal, with Balbo being accused of anti-Semitism.

In addition to Libya, the island of Rhodes, in the eastern Mediterranean, was occupied by Italy after the Balkan Wars of 1912. Until the 1930s the largely Sephardic Jewish population there ran its own internal affairs, but with the creation of the Union of Jewish Communities it too came under the centralized power of the Fascist state.

The stage was now set for the march towards war.

Recommended Readings

Bernardini, Paolo. "The Jews in Nineteenth Century Italy." *Journal of Modern Italian Studies* I:2 (1996): 292-310.

De Felice, Renzo. *The Jews in Fascist Italy: A History*. New York: Enigma Books, 2001.

Sarfatti, Michele. *The Jews in Mussolini's Italy*. Madison: University of Wisconsin Press, 2006.

Segre, Dan. "The Emancipation of Jews in Italy," in *Paths of Emancipation: Jews, States, and Citizenship*, ed. Pierre Birnbaum & Ira Katznelson. Princeton: Princeton University Press, 1995, 206-237.

Zimmerman, Joshua D., ed. *Jews in Italy under Fascist and Nazi Rule, 1922-1945*. New York: Cambridge University Press, 2005.

Timeline

GENERAL		JEWISH
Manifesto of Racist Scientists	July 1938	
Rome-Berlin Axis	Oct 1938	Jews expelled from academies, cultural institutions
Racial Laws	Sept/Nov 1938	Expulsion from universities, schools
"Pact of Steel"	May 1939	
	June 1939	Jews banned from professions
Nazi Invasion of Poland: Beginning of World War II	Sept 1939	DELASEM
Italy joins the War: Invasion of France	June 1940	Roman Jews vending licenses revoked
Italian invasion of Egypt via Libya	Sept 1940	
Rommel and Afrika Korps	1941	
Yugoslavia falls	April 1941	
"Operation Barbarossa"	June 1941	
Pearl Harbor	Dec 1941	
Battle of El Alamein	Oct. 1942	
"Operation Torch"	Nov 11, 1942—Jan 1943	
Badoglio's 45 days	Sept 8, 1943	
	Sept 26	50 kilos of gold—Roman Jews
	Oct 16	Razzia of Rome
Police order #5	Nov 1943	
Ardeatine Caves massacre	March 24, 1944	
Rome liberated	June 4, 1944	
End of Nazi control in Italy	April 1945	

Chapter 7

WORLD WAR II

In his new search for allies, Mussolini turned northward to the Nazi government of Adolph Hitler. In October 1938 the two signed the "Rome-Berlin Axis," which was consolidated in May 22, 1939 with the signing of the "Pact of Steel." However, Mussolini bided his time to join the war until June 1940, when Germany successfully invaded France.

Initially, when Hitler had come to power, Mussolini had acted against the Nazis and their anti-Semitic actions by opening the borders of Italy and allowing Jews to settle within his country. He had also opened universities to European Jews, hoping to influence them politically, and indeed students from Hungary, Rumania, and Poland came to study. Once Italy invaded Ethiopia, however, things changed. Mussolini became anti-Zionist, declaring that he would not tolerate divided loyalties, and by 1936, anti-Zionism in the newspapers became anti-Semitism. The creation of the Axis changed things completely, solidifying Mussolini's attitude toward the Jews. Without pressure from Hitler, Mussolini, between September and November of 1938, promulgated the Racial Laws, which aimed at forcing the Jews of Italy out of the country.

**Provisions for the Defense of the Italian Race,
Royal Legal Decree of November 17, 1938**

Chapter 1. Measures Relating to Marriage

Art. 1. Marriage between an Italian citizen of the Aryan race and a person belonging to another race is forbidden. A marriage celebrated despite such prohibition is null and void.

Art. 2. Whereas the prohibition in Art.1 remains in effect, the marriage of an Italian citizen with a person of foreign nationality is subordinate to the consent of the Minister for Internal Affairs. Transgressors will be sentenced to up to three months in prison and a fine of up to 10,000 lire.

Art. 3. Whereas the prohibition in Art. 1 still remains in effect, the employees of civil and military state administration, of the organizations of the National Fascist Party or those under its control, of the provincial administration, of the municipalities, of state-controlled entities and of unions and collateral agencies cannot enter in marriage with persons of a foreign nationality....

Art. 6. Marriages celebrated in violation of Art.1, shall not be civilly valid and must not, therefore, be entered into the records of the civil registry....

Chapter 2. On Those Belonging to the Jewish Race.

Art. 8. For legal purposes:

a.] those born of parents who are both of the Jewish race, even if belonging to religions different from the Jewish religion, are considered of the Jewish race;

b.] those born of parents of which one is of the Jewish race and the other of foreign nationality, are considered of the Jewish race;

c.] those born of a mother of the Jewish race, if the father is unknown, are considered of the Jewish race;

d.] Those even though born to parents of Italian nationality, of which only one is of the Jewish race, or belonging to the Jewish religion, or registered in a Jewish community, or have manifested, in any other way, indications of Judaism, are considered of the Jewish race.

e.] Those born of parents of Italian nationality, of which only one is of the Jewish race, who at the date of October 1, 1938, belonged to a religion other than the Jewish religion, are not considered of the Jewish race.

Art. 9. Those belonging to the Jewish race must be declared and entered in the records of the Registrar of births, deaths, and marriages and the bureau of vital records....

Art. 10. Italian citizens of the Jewish race may not:

a.] serve in the military in times of peace or war;

b.] act as guardian for minors or disabled people who do not belong to the Jewish race;

c.] be owners or managers, with whatever title, of businesses declared as being of interest to the National defense, ... nor of a business of any nature which employs one hundred or more persons, ...

d.] be owners of land which, in total, has a value of more than five thousand lire;

e.] be owners of urban buildings which, in total, have an assessable tax of more than twenty thousand lire....

Art. 11. A parent of the Jewish race may be deprived of parental authority over children who belong to a religion different from the Jewish religion, if it is proved that they give them an education which does not correspond to their religious principles or to the national purpose.

Art. 12. Those belonging to the Jewish race may not have in their employment any domestics who are Italian citizens of the Aryan race...

Art. 13. The following may not have persons belonging to the Jewish race in their employment:

a.] Civil and Military State Administrations;

b.] The PNF and the organizations depending upon it or under its control;

c.] The Administrations of the Provinces, of the Municipalities, of Public Institutions of Charity and of Boards, Institutes and Businesses....

d.] The Administrations of Municipal establishments;

e.] The Administrations of State controlled institutions....

g.] The Administrations of banks of national interest;

h.] The Administrations of private insurance firms.

Art. 14. The Minister for Internal Affairs, on the documented application of the interested parties, may, case by case, declare the applicability of Art.s 10 and 11....

a.] to the members of families of those who died in the Libyan, World, Ethiopian, and Spanish wars and of those who died for the Fascist cause;

b.] to those who find themselves in the following conditions:

1. maimed, disabled, wounded, war volunteers, or holders of a decoration from the Libyan, World, Ethiopian, and Spanish Wars;

2. servicemen in the Libyan, World, Ethiopian, and Spanish Wars, who have at least obtained a war cross medal of valor....

Art. 17. It is prohibited for foreign Jews to take up residence in the Kingdom, in Libya and in the Aegean possessions.

Chapter 3. Temporary and final regulations

Art. 20. The employees of the institutes mentioned in Art. 13, who belong to the Jewish race, will be released from service within three months from the effective date of the present decree....

Art. 23. Italian citizenship already granted to foreign Jews after January 1, 1919, is revoked in all cases.

Art. 24.Foreign Jews and those to whom Art. 23 applies, those who began their residence in the Kingdom, in Libya, and in the Aegean possessions after January 1, 1919, must leave the territory of the Kingdom before March 12, 1939. Those who do not comply with this obligation within the said term will be arrested for up to three months or fined up to 5,000 lire....

Art. 25. The enforcement of Art. 24 does not apply to Jews of foreign nationality who, prior to October 1, 1938:

a.] have reached the sixty-fifth year of age;

b.] have married a person of Italian citizenship....

Art. 27. Nothing is changed regarding the public practice of religion and the activity of the Jewish communities, according to the laws in effect, except the modifications in case of the need to coordinate such laws with the dispositions of the present decree....

Art. 29. The King's Government is authorized to issue regulations necessary for the implementation of the present decree. The present decree will be presented to Parliament for its conversion into law. The DUCE, Minister of Internal Affairs, as proponent, is authorized to present the attached bill. We order that the present decree, sealed with the State Seal, be inserted in the official body of laws and decrees of the Kingdom of Italy, imposing on everyone to observe them and to see that they are observed.

Rome, November 17, 1938
Victor Emmanuel
Mussolini—Ciano-Solmi—DeRevel--Lantani

(Italian, cited in Renzi De Felice, *Storia degli ebrai italiani sotto fascismo.* Turin: Einaudi, 1972, 562-66.)

The groundwork had been laid the previous year by two anti-Semitic incidents. The first was when Paolo Orana, Parliament member and rector of the University of Perugia, published (probably with Mussolini's approval), an article entitled "The Jews of Italy," which outlined a specifically Italian brand of Fascist anti-Semitism. This was not based on eugenics or biology, like Hitler's own anti-Semitism, but rather on religious, historical, and national considerations. He concluded that the Jews themselves brought about anti-Semitism by their behavior, for they never assimilated. A second incident was when the government sponsored the publishing of the *Manifesto of Racist Scientists* on July 14, 1938. This book was a blatantly anti-Semitic tract, and described the Jews as a non-European race which was widely distributed throughout Italy.

Mussolini's move to racial anti-Semitism throughout 1938 was the result of a complicated series of small and then larger steps. One important new factor in this mix was the influence of a new generation of advisers, raised in a Fascist environment with no personal memories of good relations with Jews. This group was more apt to buy into the anti-Jewish propaganda that Jews by definition had dual loyalties.

The press was given the job of psychologically preparing the public for anti-Semitism. Radio broadcasts also played a role. The Union of Jewish Communities was in disarray, with no unified leadership, and unable to face down the rising tide of propaganda. Many Jews thought that the virulence would pass, and so the *Manifesto of Racist Scientists* took them by surprise. They were wounded to the core.

The two possible obstacles that Mussolini had to contend with in his march to racial anti-Semitism were the king and the pope. The king's concern was specifically for Italian Jews, especially those who had served in the Italian armed forces during World War I. Pope Pius XI was mainly concerned about Jews who had converted and married Italian Christians. Mussolini incorporated both of these concerns and modified the Racial Laws before promulgating them.

The first of the Racial Laws was passed on September 5, 1938, and stated that Italian Jews could not send their children to Italian schools or be employed by schools, from kindergarten through university. This followed the expulsion of all foreign Jewish students earlier that year. The law affected an additional 4,400 Jewish children in elementary schools, 1,000 in secondary schools, and 200 in universities. The response to this law was an overwhelming silence though over a hundred professors were expelled, including leading scientists, many of whom left the country to search for jobs elsewhere. Jews were also excluded from the Italian academies, which were the major cultural institutions of the country. To this as well there was silence and even indifference on the part of the Italian intellectuals. On November 15, the law was expanded to remove all textbooks by Jewish authors from all schools.

An even more significant anti-Semitic law, entitled "Laws for the Defense of the Race," was passed by the Council of Ministers and signed by both Mussolini and King Victor Emanuel III on November 17, 1938. Intermarriages of any sort were henceforth illegal, and children of intermarriages could not be educated in Judaism. Jews were banned from serving in the military, barred from any state employment, and forbidden to own any business with over one hundred employees. Jews could not own sizeable tracts of land or urban buildings of value. No non-Jewish domestic servants could be employed by Jews. Citizenship granted to Jews after 1919 was revoked, and all foreign Jews—except those married to Italian citizens or over sixty-five year of age—had to leave Italy within four months.

Still another group of laws of this nature, passed June 29, 1939, banned Jews from professions such as medicine, dentistry, engineering, law, and journalism. They could not use newspapers for death notices, own radios, publish books, or have their names in telephone books. All of these laws applied to the Jews of Italian colonies as well.

> **Giorgio Bassani**
> **(1916-2000)**
>
> Born in Bologna to a wealthy Ferrara family, Giorgio Bassani studied literature, history, and philosophy, graduating from the University of Bologna just as the 1938 Racial Laws were being introduced into Italy. As a Jew, he could not publish and his work opportunities were very limited, so he taught at the Jewish School of Ferrara and published his first book under a pseudonym. He was active in the anti-Fascist resistance group in Ferrara and was arrested in May 1943, to be released two months later after Mussolini was ousted. Moving to Rome, he began his long and successful literary career as a novelist, poet, essayist, editor and intellectual. His most famous book was *The Garden of the Finzi Continis* (1962), in which he described the Italian Jewish community of Ferrara under Fascism in a complex analytic narrative style which exposes the difficulties of searching for truth in memory and moral conscience.

The reaction among the Jewish community was varied. About 6,000 Jews emigrated, especially the intellectuals and middle class, making their way to Argentina, Brazil, Palestine, and Britain. A few moved to the United States. Over 3,500 Jews converted to Catholicism, thinking that this would save them, and also thinking that the situation had to change eventually. The remainder tried to continue with their lives and adapt to the harsh situation. The laws were felt less acutely by the majority of the Jews of Rome, who still lived in the ghetto area. They were mainly lower class economically, and were also less educated and more traditional than other Italian Jews. Since they had not climbed very high on the social ladder, they were less affected by the restrictive laws until June 1940, when the street vending licenses were revoked. This effectively removed the Roman Jews' only means of earning a living.

In June 1940, after France fell to the Germans and the collaborationist Vichy Government was in place to rule its southern region, Mussolini declared war. He and Hitler had divided up the theaters of war, with Italy in charge of the entire Mediterranean, both the European and North African sectors. Later, they also divided up the Balkans and the Middle East. In September, Italy invaded Egypt from Libya in an attempt to destroy the British and take over the Suez Canal, but by December the British began an offensive action there. As a result, in early 1941 Hitler sent General Erwin Rommel to Libya with his *Afrika Korps* to salvage that front. Meanwhile, Germany invaded Yugoslavia and Greece and divided the conquered area among Germany, Italy, and Bulgaria, which had joined the war on the Axis side.

With Germany focusing on the invasion of Russia starting in June 1941, and the United States joining the war as a result of the attack on Pearl Harbor by the Japanese on December 7, 1941, World War II expanded. Rommel took all of Libya in January 1942 and proceeded eastward to Egypt and the Suez Canal. He was stopped in October of that year by an Allied army commanded by General Montgomery. The Battle of El Alamein was a turning point in the war, for within a few months of the German defeat there the Allies launched "Operation Torch," invading both Morocco and Algeria, and heading for Tunisia. North Africa fell to the Allies in January 1943, and the Allies decided to invade Europe via Sicily.

In Italy, although the Racial Laws were officially in place, the Italians were not necessarily obeying them. In every country or territory which

Italy was occupying, whether it was Croatia, western Greece, southern France, Libya, or Tunisia, the army refused to have the Jews deported. In Libya, Balbo mitigated the Racial Laws by applying them only to the small number of Italian Jews in that country. Italian military officers may have gone along with the idea of interning Jews, but they absolutely refused to ship them northward to Poland or Germany, where they knew that death awaited them. Some helped passively by allowing Jews to seek refuge; others actively protected them. Those officers who refused to do so wrote memoranda which went up the chain of command of both the foreign ministry and the armed forces. The main ploy used was delaying and obstructing in a play for time. When interviewed after the war and asked why they did this, the officers shrugged their Italian shrugs and said that theirs was a simple act of humanitarianism, and that war was against soldiers, not against civilians. As scholar Susan Zuccotti wrote:

> They ignored Mussolini's directives, occasionally with his tacit consent. They neglected to pass on instruction, made orders deliberately vague and imprecise, invented absurd bureaucratic excuses, lied, and totally misled the Germans. If the subject had not been so serious and the stakes so desperately high, the story might have acquired the dimensions of a comic opera, with befuddled Germans concluding, as usual, that Italians were blatant liars and hopelessly incompetent administrators. But thousands of lives were at stake and the game was stark and deadly. (Zuccotti, "The Italians and the Holocaust," 75)

Yugoslavia capitulated in April 1941. Italy was granted the Dalmatian coast and control of the western military occupation zone of Croatia. That summer the Ustasha, or Croatian Fascist Party, under Ante Pavelic, began to kill both Jews and Serbs. The Italians protected the Jews and refused to turn them over to the Germans, who appealed to Mussolini. The Duce "did not object" to deportations of Jews; however he sent no detailed instructions, thus delaying any action. By 1943 it became more difficult to protect the Jews, and thus many went into hiding. Between 2,200 and 3,000 Jews survived in this area.

Greece too was divided in 1941. Germany took over Crete, Macedonia, and Thrace, including the city of Salonika with its large Jewish population. Italy got the Ionic islands and much of the Greek peninsula, including Athens with its 13,000 Jews. Italy claimed all Jews of Italian origin in

Salonika, and gave naturalization papers to Jews married to Greeks as well as to "wives" of Italian soldiers. However, when Germany took over in 1943, it deported thousands of Jews from Athens, Rhodes, Corfu, and Crete, and almost the entire community of Salonika.

Southern France was Vichy-controlled until November 11, 1942, when the Allies invaded North Africa. Italy then occupied eight departments, or provinces, east of the Rhone and proceeded to protect both French and foreign Jews. Word quickly spread about the protection and safety offered by Italian rule, and the Jewish population of this area rose from about 20,000 to 50,000 within a year. Most of the Jews were in Nice, from which they were sent to enforced residence in villages, similar to what was done in Italy, as shall be discussed shortly.

The Jews inside Italy turned inward, as they had centuries earlier at the time of the creation of ghettos. The leadership of the Union was overhauled at the end of 1939, and an energetic new president, Dante Almansi, took control. The Jews set up their own schools, tapping the talents of the fired teachers and university professors who remained in Italy. The university

DELASEM

Delegazione per l'Assistenza deghli Emigranti Ebrei (The Delegation for the Assistance of Jewish Emigrants) was a Jewish resistance organization in Italy from 1939 to 1947. Organized in December 1939 by leaders of the Union of Jewish Communities and authorized by the Fascist government, its purpose was to help foreign Jews interned in Italy to emigrate.

DELASEM's headquarters was in Genoa, and its director was Lelio Vittoria Valobra. Funds came at first through Paris and then through Switzerland, from institutions such as the American Jewish Joint Distribution Committee and the Hebrew Immigrant Aid Society. From 1939 to September 1943, when the Nazis took over northern Italy, DELASEM helped 5,000 Jews leave the country and provided aid to Jews held in internment camps. When the occupation began, DELASEM Jewish leaders went underground, giving leadership power to Cardinal Pietro Boetto of Genoa and his secretary Francesco Repetto. Aid continued to be funneled to Jews. In Rome, the Jewish leaders worked with the Capuchin Father Maria Benedetto. Money was distributed, along with false documents; hiding places were also found for Jews.

After the war, the priority task of DELASEM was to bring together scattered families, especially by searching for children hidden in Catholic institutions or private homes. It was also active in organizing emigration to Palestine.

students thus continued their studies, using private book collections since they were no longer permitted to use the public ones. They organized relief work for foreign Jews setting up the Delgazione Assistenza Emigranti Ebrei (DELASEM) in 1939. With the start of the war, this group began to help Italian Jews as well. Unemployment led to poverty for many, and by 1941, as was mentioned in the case of Rome, even the Jewish peddlers lost their licenses. DELASEM collaborated with the Italian authorities who were happy to be relieved of both the burden of foreign Jews and the needs of Italian Jews. DELASEM also brought in foreign currency, via international Jewish organizations such as the Joint Distribution Committee. These funds were funneled into Italy via Switzerland after the United States entered the war. DELASEM also functioned in the Italian-occupied zones, where one of its most outstanding actions was cooperating in the rescue of dozens of children housed in Villa Emma.

Villa Emma

As Nazi control spread to the Balkans in 1942, there was an attempt to rescue as many Jewish children there as possible. Over one hundred children of mixed national backgrounds were sent into Italy and housed in Villa Emma in the town of Nonantola, near Modena, where they were supported by DELASEM. The children were not regarded as internees and so could move about in the town freely. The house was run like a Jewish Italian boarding school, with classes given in Hebrew language and Jewish culture as well as secular subjects. Meals were mainly vegetarian, and basic necessities like second-hand clothing and shoes were provided by DELASEM. The children were also taught farming, as the Zionist dream of their leaders was to settle in Palestine.

In September 1943, as Nazi forces moved into northern Italy, DELASEM was involved in rescuing these children again, this time by evacuating them from Villa Emma and hiding them among local families and Catholic institutions until they could be taken on the dangerous journey to neutral Switzerland. Father Arrigo Beccari was a major figure in the rescue, as were Giuseppi Moreali and Goffredo Pacifici.

All of the children—except for one sick boy who was in a sanatorium—were saved. Most ended up in Palestine after the war was over.

The majority of Italian Jews, however, managed on their own. Though they were officially forbidden, friendships with Italians continued, and even though it was forbidden to have non-Jewish servants, many servants surreptitiously continued to do their work. Because of the law against ritual slaughter, observant Jews did not eat meat. Synagogues were overflowing. Life was hard in the cities, but relatively bearable.

Life was also bearable for those Jews in internal exile. These were people sent to live in the countryside, under a kind of house arrest. The experiences of these Jews varied, as some towns and their police forces treated them well and others did not. By 1942 there were 5,000 Jews in internal exile.

In the Italian concentration camps, which had been established when the War began, things were harder, because there was little food, poor shelter, and crude hygiene. The internees organized themselves, sometimes creating what became almost miniature cities: raising crops, installing plumbing and public baths, setting up synagogues and schools, and even planning cultural events. By 1942, there were about 3,500 Jews in these camps.

As a result of the Allied invasion of Sicily, Mussolini was overthrown, and Marshal Pietro Badoglio became prime minister and declared an armistice, assuming that the Allies would rapidly move northward. He ordered the Italian army to lay down its arms, but the only Allied forces on the Italian mainland on September 8 were those of the Eighth British Army, led by General Montgomery, which had landed at Messina. The eighteen German army divisions in northern Italy and along the northern borders waited for this surrender to make their move. After 45 days of Badoglio's rule, the Nazis moved in to take over northern and central Italy. The Badoglio government had taken no real initiative regarding the Jews, other than those in southern France, which they had protected as they had the Jews of Croatia, perhaps because of a lack of time. Badoglio had not even destroyed his lists of Jewish names, despite appeals to do so. The Nazis rescued Mussolini and set him up as a puppet ruler of the newly-named "Italian Social Republic," in its capital, Salo; but the Nazis were now making all of the decisions. They also took over all of the Italian occupied zones. For the first few months there were no deportations from the occupied zones, but that changed, bringing Nazi activity in line with what was going to take place in Italy itself. For example, when Badoglio fell, Germany entered Nice and the Jews fled to the mountains. The Nazi manhunt was more successful in this area than in others that had been under Italian control.

On September 26, the Jews of Rome were given an order to collect fifty kilograms of gold, but had only thirty-six hours in which to do so. The Jews rushed about, seeking aid from non-Jews as well, thinking that raising this amount of gold would keep them safe. They were wrong, as the demand was only a ruse. On October 13, the Germans confiscated the library of the Roman synagogue, with its manuscripts, incunabula, prints, and unique books, and shipped the volumes to Germany. Although the gold was raised, the first *razzia*, or roundup, of Jews took place on October 16. In nine hours 1,259 Jews—a tenth of the Roman Jewish population—were arrested. The cities of Milan, Turin, Florence, Siena, Bologna, Venice, Mantua, and Genoa quickly followed, and by December four deportation trains had headed northward to Poland. The Nazis used the Italian Jewish community records to track down the Jews listed. It is estimated that by the end of the war 8,500 Italian Jews had been deported. Others were killed in raids and individual massacres, such as those at Val D'Aosta and Lake Maggiore. Seventy-five Jews died in the massacre in the Ardeatine Caves, outside Rome, on March 24, 1944.

There was only one extermination camp set up on Italian soil. It was near Trieste, a part of Italy that had long been under Austrian control and had been influenced by Austrian anti-Semitism. This camp was in San Sabba, in an old rice factory; it actually contained a crematorium. There were about thirty provincial concentration camps, but they were used to intern people, not to kill them. A main one was at Fossoli, near Bologna, and another earlier one was at Ferramonti in Calabria. It is estimated that about 2,000 people died in the San Sabba camp: some of them were Jews, but others were partisans or other enemies of the state.

By the end of November 1943, police order number five was announced, ordering the arrest and internment of all Jews. There was usually task-sharing involved in these actions: the Italians arrested the Jews, and the Germans deported them. Only in the two regions of German-occupied northern Italy did the Germans do both. These regions were renamed *Alpenvorland* (which included the provinces of Bolzano, Trento, and Bellino) and *Adriatisches Kustenland* (which included the provinces of Trieste, Gorizia, Fiume, Poli, and Lubiana). In these regions, the German military authorities, aided by collaborationist local people, got to work rounding up as many Jews as they could find. The *razzia* in Trieste took place on Yom Kippur, October 9, 1943. Those who had not managed to flee or hide were caught.

The Nazis arrived on the island of Rhodes in February 1944. Neutral Turkey tried to save as many Jews there as it could, claiming that they were Turkish citizens. In July, 2,780 Jews were rounded up and shipped to Greece, where they were added to the convoys of Salonika Jews; they all ended up in Auschwitz and Birkenau. On June 4, 1944, Rome was liberated by the Allies, and by April 1945 all of Italy was free of Nazi control.

Between 75% and 85% of Italy's Jews survived the Holocaust. Scholars have addressed the question of how this number remained so high, and have come up with a list of factors that contributed to the high rate of survival. The first item is that the deportation and killing of Jews began late, as until September 1943 not the Nazis but the Italians were in control. Another contributing factor is that the Jews hid once the roundups began, and they knew that the Allies were on their way. Hope and courage are not unimportant to survival. In addition, the danger period was short as compared to that in other countries: one year in Rome and Florence, and about 20 months in the north. Then there are the specific characteristics of Italian Jews to be considered: they were few in number, only one-tenth of one percent, and therefore sympathetic Christians could handle their needs for shelter, food, and documents. Most Italian Jews had some financial resources, and most looked Italian, spoke Italian, and had friendships and contacts with non-Jews, all of which enabled them to pass for Italian once the Nazis took over control. They were still in good health and were relatively young, and they had friends and contacts. Intangible factors include the amiable inclination of the Italians to ignore the law, especially if they felt that it was imposed on them by the Germans. Italian peasants tend to be known for their independent thinking and sense of justice. Also, like other Italians, Jews tended to be very individualistic: they lived by their own wits and resources, found their own rescuers, and dealt with individuals. The decision to commit oneself to rescuing Jews was an emotional decision, one that was spontaneous, uncalculated, and often even irrational. It was helpful that in Italy there was almost no tradition of modern anti-Semitism, and that Italian culture as a whole tended toward altruism. Luck, of course, played its role as well.

In other words, the road to survival was very complex and involved a combination of innate cultural characteristics, individual commitment, and political considerations. The one topic in this area that has been explored in great depth is the role of the Catholic Church and the Pope during World War II. Most scholars agree that both Pope Pius XI and Pope Pius XII were anti-Judaism, but that they were not believers in racial

Primo Levi
(1919-1987)

Born in Turin into an intellectual middle-class Jewish family, Primo Levi excelled academically from a very young age and was accepted at the University of Turin to study chemistry. Because he began his studies in 1937, he was allowed to complete them despite the Racial Laws which prohibited Jews from attending state schools. He graduated in 1941, but could not find a permanent job. The upheavals of the fall of Mussolini, the brief Badoglio armistice, and the Nazi invasion of northern Italy directly affected him. He went into hiding and joined the Italian partisans, but was captured by the Fascist militia. As a Jew, he was sent to an internment camp at Fossoli, near Modena. But when Fossoli was taken over by the Nazis in February 1944, the Jews were transported to Auschwitz, where Levi spent eleven months until it was liberated in January 1945. He was one of twenty Italian Jews to survive Auschwitz, in part because he was put to work indoors in a laboratory that aimed at producing synthetic rubber and in part because he was sick in the infirmary when the SS forced most Jews to begin the death march of January 1945. He returned to Turin in October 1945 after a long circuitous railroad trip through eastern Europe.

Primo Levi found work as a chemist, but also began writing about his experiences during World War II. By the end of 1946 he had completed *If This is a Man* (known in the United States as *Survival at Auschwitz*), which was published in 1947. He worked and wrote until 1977, when he retired and devoted himself full-time to writing memoirs, short stories, poems, novels, and essays, becoming a major literary figure. He also believed passionately in bearing witness to the horrors of Nazism. He died in 1987, either by an accidental fall or by committing suicide. One of his most famous works is *The Periodic Table* (1975).

anti-Semitism. In fact, Pope Pius XI wrote an encyclical condemning anti-Semitism at the end of 1938, but suffered a heart attack in November of that year, and died in February 1939, before he could deliver it. The new pope, Pius XII, wanted to keep the peace and refused to take an open stand on the Jewish issue. It is claimed by some that his silence saved lives. If it did, it also certainly compromised the moral stature of the Vatican.

According to scholars who intensively researched this question, the pope never issued any kind of rescue order—neither written nor oral—to members of Church. There is also no written evidence that he ordered the opening of Church institutions to Jewish fugitives. If Church institutions such as monasteries and convents hid Jews, it was because of the spontaneous actions of individual Catholics. If anything, the Vatican disapproved of such actions. As for the archbishops of Genoa, Turin, Florence, and Milan, who helped the Jews, they did so because of direct requests from local committees of DELASEM and their own personalities. Outstanding among them was Pietro Boetto the archbishop of Genoa, his secretary Don Francesco Repetto, and the French Capuchin Father Maria Benedetto (Benoit-Marie) in Rome. These three managed DELASEM beginning in March 1944, when the Jews who had been doing so had to flee for their lives. The local priests, nuns, and monks who acted did not need a papal directive to do so, nor did they have to apprise the Vatican of their actions. The bottom line is that Pope Pius XII was not directly involved in the rescue of Jews in any way.

The other side of the question is, how did Italy allow 15%-25% of its Jews to be transported to their deaths? The Nazi war machine was part of the answer, as was the inability of the Italian armed forces to resist Nazi power: any Italian caught helping the Jews was arrested and executed. Additionally, especially in the area around Trieste, Italian fascists were as anti-Semitic as the Nazis were.

The Holocaust in Italy was not a minor event, even though the numbers of Italian Jews were small when compared to the numbers of Polish Jews. There was not a single Jew who was not affected, who did not lose family and friends, or who did not feel that their government, their neighbors, and their countrymen had betrayed them.

Recommended Reading

De Felice, Renzo. *The Jews in Fascist Italy, a History*. New York: Enigma Books, 2001.

Pugliese, Stanislao, ed. *The Most Ancient of Minorities*. Westport, CT: Greenwood Press, 2002.

Sarfatti, Michele. *The Jews in Mussolini's Italy*. Madison: University of Wisconsin Press, 2006.

Stille, Alexander. *Benevolence and Betrayal: Five Italian Jewish Families under Fascism*. New York: Summit Books, 1991.

Zimmerman, Joshua D., ed. *Jews in Italy under Fascist and Nazi Rule, 1922-1945*. New York: Cambridge University Press, 2005.

Zuccotti, Susan. *The Italians and the Holocaust: Persecution, Rescue, Survival*. New York: Basic Books, 1987.

Timeline

GENERAL		JEWISH
	1941	First meeting of Italian synagogue congregation in Jerusalem
World War II ends	1945	Illegal immigration into mandate Palestine begins
United Nations votes in favor of partition of Palestine into two states	29 Nov 1947	
State of Israel declared	May 14/15, 1948	
Libyan independence under King Idris	1951	Conegliano Veneto synagogue dismantled and shipped to Jerusalem to become the Italian synagogue (in the old German Compound)
Six Day War	1967	Libyan Jews begin to arrive in Italy
Qadhafi in Libya	Oct 1969	Libyan Jews flee to Italy in greater numbers
Overthrow of Shah of Iran by Ayatolah Khomeini	1978	Persian Jews arrive in Italy
Collapse of Soviet Union	1991	Russian Jews arrive in Italy
	1997	Irani Jews open social club in Milan

Chapter 8

CONTEMPORARY ITALY

When the war ended, most of the Jews of Italy who had been uprooted—whether by deportation, flight, or incarceration in labor camps—and survived, returned to their homes. Anyone who had confiscated their property, whether private homes or businesses, had to return this property according to Italian law. In smaller communities, everyone knew everyone, and so even confiscated furniture was returned. Property of synagogues, art collections, and libraries that had survived and not been shipped north to Germany were also returned.

The post-war Italian governments made quiet efforts to identify old synagogues that were no longer in use, mostly those in small cities, and then shipped the defunct synagogues' contents to Israel, where they were re-used in a number of locations: in Heichal Shlomo in Jerusalem, in the Italian Synagogue in Jerusalem, and in various other synagogues around the country. The Italian government also quietly aided Italian Jews who moved to the newly created State of Israel, enabling them to buy apartments and set up small businesses. These unassuming activities were part of the reason why few or no reparations claims were made to the postwar Italian governments.

With the war over, Italian Jews began to pick up the threads of their lives, but with their small numbers and high rate of intermarriage, as well as the lure of the newly created State of Israel, it looked as though the community would eventually disappear. Remarkably, this did not happen. The community's survival was in part due to the same demographic factor that had affected Italian Jews throughout the centuries: new Jews from various countries began to arrive. Small numbers of Ashkenazi Jews appeared, but it was two Middle Eastern Jewish groups that came in large enough numbers to make a difference. These were the Jews of Libya and the Jews of Iran.

Tradition has it that both communities date back to the period of the Second Temple. With the exception of a brief period of Christian occupation, Libya came under Arab and then Ottoman Turkish control until 1911. Libyan Jews were treated as *Dhimmi*, and their most common economic pursuits were trade, both maritime and caravan, and metal-working; there were also many silk spinners and weavers, as well as dyers. The community as a whole was poor, with the wealth in the hands of a few families.

The nineteenth century saw the beginnings of modernization and westernization for Libyan Jews, through both the arrival of European Jewish settlers and the subsequent opening of both Italian-Jewish schools and Alliance Israelite Universelle schools in addition to the more traditional Hebrew and rabbinical schools. One the eve of the Italian occupation in 1911, the community was already divided between a small, rich, westernized group and the masses of poor traditional Jews. In addition, the traditional economic symbiotic relationship between the Jews and the Arabs was changing as a result of westernization, and the Jews were becoming merely intermediaries between the old society and the new. Life became more insecure, and so the Jews (each group for its own reasons) as a whole favored the Italian occupation, further affecting intercommunity relations.

It should be noted that no matter how "modern" the Libyan Jews became, until the mid-twentieth century they remained Libyans as well as Jews, thus retaining strong links to local traditions. The Italian Racial Laws—in force in Italy beginning in 1938 and extended to Libya in October 1942—and the British invasion and occupation (from 1943 to December 1951), were major turning points for Libyan Jews. Libyan nationalism grew at this time, and was imbued from the start with anti-Zionist ideas, which easily slipped into anti-Jewish ideas. Thus in the years between the creation of the State of Israel and independence of Libya under King Idris in December 1951, more than 31,000 Libyan Jews emigrated directly to Israel (or indirectly via Italy). The 6,000 that remained behind, mainly in Tripoli, are the ones who eventually moved to Italy.

Most of those who stayed were the richest and most westernized members of the society, linked to the Arab elite and the Italian minority. They had economic interests in Libya and often had Italian or other European citizenship. They had trust in King Idris' ability to rule and in his realization that he needed the Jews. The king did realize that this numerically small group had few political ambitions, was loyal, and was economically active.

Culturally, they were part of Libya and could serve as a conduit to Italy. Nonetheless, between 1952 and 1969, the Libyan government became more repressive toward the Jews, mainly because of the influence of the more radical Arabs in the Arab-Israel conflict. A crisis was reached during the Six Day War of June 1967, when demonstrations and riots began in Tripoli against the Jews. The majority of the Jews saw exodus as the only immediate solution, and by September there were only 100 Jews left; almost all of the others had moved to Italy.

The American Jewish Joint Distribution Committee, as part of its traditional international role of helping Jews, had the task of receiving and helping the Libyan Jews. The United Nations High Commissioner for Refugees participated, but the United Hebrew Immigrant Aid Society and the AJDC assumed most of the expenses and relations with international organizations. The Union of Italian Jewish Communities took care of relations with Italian authorities. The Deputazione Israelitica di Assistenza (Jewish Aid Committee) of the community of Rome took care of the refugees in the capital, and the refugees set up their own emergency committee representing them in all of their dealings.

Some refugees—1,200 people or 230 families—who were Italian citizens with funds available in Italy made their own arrangements, and most of them settled in Rome. Some 200 families, or 1,000 people, went temporarily to the three refugee camps in Latina, Capua, and outside Naples, and for the most part subsequently left for Israel. A third group of about 1,900 people, or 365 families, went to Rome, where the DIA assumed responsibility for most of them, giving them money and helping them find work and schools. Within a year, about 105 families (580 people) left for Israel. The goal of the community of Rome, after a year, was to integrate Libyan Jews and to solve the related religious and aid problems.

A key problem was how to recoup their holding in Libya. By travelling back and forth many Libyan Jews did recoup a good part of their holdings, but some Jews with large amounts of property and wealth did not manage to do so by the time of the military coup d'etat in September 1969 and Mu'ammar Qadhafi's takeover in October. In July 1970, Qadhafi adopted a series of anti-Jewish measures, including sequestering assets of Jews residing overseas permanently without compensation. This occurred at the same time that all traces of foreign presence were being removed from Libya.

The Jews of Libyan origin living in Italy today reside mainly in Rome. They number roughly 3,000 people (taking into account that this number is becoming more difficult to assess with the rise in intercommunal marriages), and have maintained a cohesive community in part by living in the same neighborhood and in part by establishing their own synagogues. The main group lives around Piazza Bologna. The Italian community put up half the money to buy the main Libyan synagogue in a renovated movie house in 1981. There are services every day, and three *minyanim* (quorums) on Saturday. Interestingly, the earliest of the three services tends to be more heavily attended by the men, averaging 100 participants. About 80 women come to the 9:30 a.m. service, and between 60 to 70 boys have a separate service upstairs. The reason for the heavy attendance at the 7 a.m. services is that most of the men then go to open their shops and businesses. On Rosh ha-Shana about 1,000 people come (including approximately 400 women), and the synagogue's highest attendance is on Yom Kippur, when over 1,000 men and 500 women are present.

In addition to serving as a center for prayer, the synagogue is also the center for evening classes for adults and a Sunday School Talmud Torah for special classes in Libyan-"style" Judaism for children ages 5-11. There is a 1,000-pupil Jewish day school in the center of Rome right near the main synagogue, but it is very expensive and not considered to be on as high a level as the Italian schools. In addition, the bus trip to the school has come to be considered a dangerous target for extremists. The topic of Jewish education is a fundamental one for Libyan Jews, as it is for Italian Jews in general. Many members of the community have opted for a public high school education, supplemented by an intensive five-hour Sunday program using a *bet medrash* method for teaching Jewish subjects to that age group.

Libyan Jews consider formal Jewish education important for Jewish continuity, but places it on an equal level with the influence of the home. Respect for parents and their wishes continues to be an important element in their world, but after forty years in Italy, the absolute power of the patriarch—let alone the matriarch—is gone. This is seen clearly in the change from the parents choosing a spouse for a child to the young person making the choice independently. Sometimes, however—and this is one of the major changes in the Libyan community—there is intermarriage. Statistical population reports show that 15% of Libyan Jews now intermarry. This seems to be happening as a result of a number of things: a larger number of Libyan Jews attending university, where they meet the Gentile majority, the falling of community barriers as each new generation becomes more Italian, and the diminishing power of parents over adult children. An interesting observation was made by an unnamed Libyan-Jewish sociologist that it is also the result of respect on the part of the Libyan men for Libyan Jewish women: premarital sex is considered disrespectful to the women involved, so Libyan Jewish university men have affairs with non-Jewish women, which sometimes lead to marriage.

While the number of Libyan Jews attending universities is growing, it is not yet comparable to the proportion of Italian Jews doing so. This is due in part to the Libyan tradition in which sons go into their father's businesses, and in part to the practical nature of these Jews, who know how difficult it is to find professional positions in Italy today. More women are moving into higher education, but many choose to attend teachers' colleges over universities. Three generations ago women married at age 15; two generations ago the age had risen to 18-20; young women today expect to defer marriage until about 25. Another major change is that most young women of today expect to work after marriage; their mothers and certainly their grandmothers—with some notable exceptions—did not. Still a further change is the decrease in the size of the family. Libyan Jews now have two to four children on average, which is much fewer than their grandparents had, although this is still a much higher birthrate than the Italian Jews and Italian Gentiles.

Libyan Jewish community leaders foresee rapid acculturation. They point to the fact that Italian was spoken in most homes even before the move to Italy. This helped immensely in the adjustment of all immigrant generations to their new country. Children could easily be placed in Italian schools, and adults did not have to struggle with a new language in the workplace or the market. That doesn't mean that it was easy to be replanted, however. Some families lost everything in Libya, and some men could find no work in Italy. Forty years have led to a strong Italianization of these Jews, yet a strong bond with Libyan customs remains, which some scholars find remarkable. Most Libyan Jews feel comfortable praying in familiar tunes and chants, eating traditional Libyan festive meals, and marrying spouses with similar customs. There has even been a revival of Libyan customs such as henna parties for brides. However, for some Jews—partly because of exposure to the other Jewish communities in Italy—intercommunal marriages are inevitable. The most important thing is to marry a Jew; if the spouse is from another Jewish community, this is not as problematic as marrying a non-Jew would be. Almost all of the people whom I interviewed identified themselves as "Italian Jews," with an emphasis on the second word; a few added "of Libyan origin."

Tullia Zevi, former president of the Italian Jewish Community, foresaw the integration of Libyan Jews into the larger community. She often lauded them for having brought "devotional wealth" to the Italian Jews and for helping revive a general interest in Jewish roots. There is no doubt about their influence on traditionalism in Italy: before the arrival of the Libyan Jews there was one kosher butcher in Rome; now there are about eight. Before the Libyan Jews came to Italy, there was a meager availability of kosher products in general, but now there is a complete kosher section in the biggest supermarket in the Piazza Bologna section of Rome. Before their arrival, use of the *miqve* or ritual bath had become almost exclusive to women of Ashkenazi origin, and now the *miqves* are in constant use by Italian Jewish and Libyan Jewish women.

Yet the danger of intermarriage lurks, and the Libyan Jewish community is fighting it by opening a private Jewish club in which young people can socialize on Saturday nights, by improving the quality and availability of classes on Jewish subjects at all levels, and by sending young people to Israel for summer vacations. There they have reconnected with relatives and family friends from Libya, and thus have reaffirmed their Jewishness as well as their "Libyan-ness."

The second Middle Eastern Jewish community to move to Italy in the past forty years comes from Iran. In stark contrast to the Jewish experience in Libya, Irani Jews lived in the extremist milieu of Shi'i Islam, which promoted the concept of the physical impurity of the *dhimmi*. Different, too, were their experiences with modernization, which really began only with the overthrow of the Qajar dynasty after World War I.

The development of political Zionism and the emergence of the state of Israel affected Irani Jews, as it did Jews in other Muslim states. Thousands moved to Israel shortly after the state was declared. Their reasons were primarily spiritual: life in Iran in the late 1940's was relatively comfortable. It remained that way until the fall of the Shah in 1978 and the rise to power of Ayatollah Khomeini and his conservative theocracy. Jews left in droves, most heading for Israel and the United States. A small group numbering a few thousand ended up in Milan, Italy.

Unlike the Libyan Jews, the Irani Jews had little knowledge of Italian, and so their initial culture shock was greater. Again unlike the Libyan Jews, the Teherani Jews generally had little Jewish education. Fifty years of modernization in Iran had led to the secularization of most Teheranis, with only some fond memories of holiday feasts and foods. As a result, most Teheranis living in Milan are rapidly acculturating to Italy and are sending their children to Italian schools that increases the rate of intermarriage. After Irani women, particularly Teherani women, are exposed to the freedom and equality of Italian women, they often want to move away from the perceived prejudicial treatment of women in Middle Eastern society.

There is one group of Irani Jews that obstinately refuses to assimilate. This is the group from Meshed, in northeastern Iran. Its history is unique, for it is made up of the descendants of a community that saw one of the few instances of forced conversions in the world of Islam, which occurred in 1839. The group converted at the time came to be known as *Jadid al-Islam* ("new" Muslims). In fact, most of them were what were elsewhere called *conversos* or secret Jews. For over 150 years some lived double lives, ensuring their continuity by marrying only within their group and piously following all the Jewish laws that they could.

Descendants of Meshdi Jews have moved to western Milan (to areas other than the center where the main Italian synagogue is located), and have recently opened their own synagogue, colloquially known as the Persian synagogue. They are gradually taking over the local Jewish school, and are importing their own Hebrew teachers from among the Meshdi Jews living in Israel. In 1997 they opened a social club (*mifgash*) for adult classes, for teenagers to gather, and for the Bnai Akiva (the religious Zionist youth group) members to hold meetings and pray. These Jews speak Judeo-Persian with the special flavor of Meshed at home, but it is solely an aural language for the young, who speak Italian, Hebrew, and often English. They pretend to go along with the central Italian Jewish community and the chief rabbi of Milan, but in fact they are following their own customs to ensure the continuity of their group. They do this through establishing their own synagogue, Jewish schools, social clubs, and neighborhood. They have even managed to retain the custom of marrying within the group. They do this through utilizing the strong ties that they maintain with Meshdi Jews throughout the world, especially in Long Island, New York; Los Angeles, California; London, England; and Jerusalem. Young people are introduced to each other in their late teens, and more often than not marry other Meshdi Jews by the time they reach their early twenties.

Only time will tell whether the tools for survival that the Jews of Meshed developed over the generations—internal cohesion, an iron determination to remain Jewish, and a traditional approach to Judaism—will continue in the new environment of Italy.

As long as Italy remains democratic and western and secular, and as long as these new Jews appear to be Italian, they will be accepted, at least in large urban areas. But most Middle Eastern Jews are not yet "insiders" in Italy, partly because not enough time has passed for them to be accepted and partly because some have chosen to retain their separateness. But over the long span of Italian-Jewish history, many different Jews have arrived in the country, and while each group has retained its different customs, its members have also become Italian Jews. Something similar will probably happen to these two groups, as well as to the even smaller groups of Lebanese Jews and Russian Jews who have recently immigrated to Italy. The difference between the historical past and the present is that now we can actually witness the process.

As for the population figures of Italian Jews, they have dropped over the past half-century to about 25,000. Rome is still the largest population by far, with about 13,500 Jews there. This is followed by Milan, with over 6,000. The numbers then plummet into the hundreds in Florence (900), Turin (875), Livorno (570), Trieste (545), Venice (455), Genoa (350), Naples (185), Bologna (185), Padua (180), Ancona (150), and Pisa (135). Cities with fewer than one hundred Jews include Mantua, Ferrara, Casalmaggiore, Merano, Modena, Parma, Vercelli, and Verona.

These numbers include only those Jews who identify themselves as such. Should intermarried couples and their children be included, the number would grow exponentially.

The predominantly urban communities, concentrated in Rome and Milan, have been deeply affected by Italian life. Still, they also retain strong institutions of religion and communal organization, and despite becoming less ritually observant, Italian Jews try to perpetuate Jewish identity and keep the High Holy Days of Rosh ha-Shana and Yom Kippur. Most are also vociferous supporters of Israel. Major personal life cycle events—

circumcisions, marriages, funerals—are community as well as individual events. They are under the control of the rabbinate, which is centered in Rome. Synagogues have youth clubs, welfare associations, adult education programs, and Talmud Torah afternoon schools. The rabbinate also supervises kosher products to guarantee their kashrut. Jewish day schools in Rome and Milan are almost as good as the best Italian schools, but attract a relatively small number of students. It is an uphill battle to convince parents that a strong Jewish education is a major weapon against intermarriage.

The long history of the Jews in Italy is one of a basic core group that arrived during the Roman Republic and then the Roman Empire, which was reinforced over the centuries by the movement to Italy of other, smaller, Jewish groups. Each new community maintained its unique identity for a time, but gradually became Italianized. The only community that managed to find a balance between its original customs and its new environment was that of the Sephardic Jews.

The experience of the Jews in Italy was both a positive and a negative one. It was positive in that there were periods of time when Jews were part of Italian culture, were tolerated in various economic fields, and had legal recourse when things went wrong. It was negative when they were persecuted by the Catholic Church, ghetto-ized, and murdered by the Nazis.

The number of Jews in Italy remains small, but it is stubbornly maintained through the arrival of new Jewish groups seeking refuge there. These are the latest communities to contribute to the Italian Jewish reputation as the most tenacious of minorities.

Recommended Reading

Della Pergola, Sergio. *Jewish and Mixed Marriages in Milan, 1901-1968.* Jerusalem: Hebrew University Press, 1972.

Focus Studies

Now that an overview of Italian Jewish history has been presented, the reader can appreciate focus studies, which cross the centuries in search of specific information. The two studies included here make use of a wide variety of primary sources. What they have in common is both the sweep of time and the cultural uniqueness of Italian Jews. The first study addresses issues of women within the world of Italian Jewish culture, and the second study addresses how a specific, very small group of Jews survived for centuries on the island of Sardinia after its members ostensibly converted to Christianity.

Chapter 9

RECLAIMING THE HEROIC JEWISH JUDITH

One of the functions of biblical figures is to serve as role models. The narrative portions of the biblical texts are rich with information which can be understood on both a literal and a more historically complex level. Throughout the millennia of Jewish history, Bible commentators have provided us with a plethora of textual readings.

In analyzing female figures, however, one sometimes finds a disparity between what the text presents and how the commentators interpret them. Interestingly, this disparity manifests itself most blatantly in connection with the strongest women, namely Sara, Deborah, and Hulda.

In Genesis XVIII, 9, when the three angels are visiting Abraham, they ask, "Where is Sara your wife? And he said: Behold in the tent (*ba-ohel*)." Rashi, living in France in 1040-1105 CE, is one of the most popular of all Jewish commentators. He explains that she was there because of modesty. That is certainly consistent with segregated roles in the ancient Middle East. But when the word *ohel* (tent) is used later to describe Jacob's location (Genesis XXV, 27), Rashi comments that he was in the "tent of Shem and Eber," meaning their houses of Torah study. Why use one explanation for Sara and another for Jacob? Could there be a gender discrepancy here?

More important than this interpretation is the destruction on the part of Rashi of the equal partnership of husband and wife, when he interprets Sarai's behavior with Hagar as one of selfishness and envy (Genesis XVI: 1-6). In interpreting Sarai's statement "My wrong be upon you," Rashi writes, "When you prayed to God you only referred to yourself as childless—you should have prayed for both of us and I too would have been remembered. Also, you wronged me by listening to what was said against me (by Hagar) and keeping silent." Why not see Sarai's actions in making her slavewoman available to be a secondary wife, with the goal of adopting her child, as generous? In the women's later disagreements, Hagar, still a slave, acted improperly in the strictly demarcated roles of the ancient Middle East. Sarai could have punished her without consulting her husband, but diplomatically asked Abram, whereupon he told her what she already knew, namely that the women of the household came under the domain of the matriarch. Hagar's behavior demanded punishment, and the angel reminded her of this by calling out, "Hagar, Sarai's slave…"

More denigrating is the treatment of Deborah (Judges IV). Not only is Deborah's role diminished, but the commentators even claim that she was chosen by God only because of the good deeds of her husband, Lapidot. No, claim these men, Deborah never really "judged," because women cannot be judges. And even her prophecy—for she is labeled a prophet in the text—was wrong, because Sisera was delivered not into her hands but into Yael's. In other words, Deborah is punished for hubris. The ultimate act of denigration is the explanation of her name, *Devorah*, stating that it is not connected with the bee, that most useful and productive of insects, but with *dabbur*, the hornet, which only stings and produces nothing positive.

This attitude is carried over to the treatment of the prophet Hulda (II Kings XXII:14-20), who lived in Jerusalem at the time of Jeremiah. She, too, is described as being chosen for prophecy due to the merits of her husband. She, too, is punished for hubris—in her case for referring to the king as "that man"—and she never has another prophecy. She, too, has the positive definition of her name changed into a negative one: *hulda* is a "cat," so important for catching rodents in the ancient Middle East, but this is changed into a "weasel," with all of the negative connotations that this animal carries.

Two post-Biblical women are also treated in a denigrating manner by later commentators. The first is Salome Alexandra (139-67 BCE), the only queen of the Hasmonean dynasty, who, it was later said, never really ruled but merely followed the decisions of her male advisors. After all, women could not have political power. The worst treatment of all was saved for Beruriah (second century CE), a scholar in her own right whose legal decisions are recorded in the Talmud. Medieval commentators describe a wager, a seduction, a suicide, and a flight. This was written a thousand years later, and is loosely based on an enigmatic phrase.

It seems that the scholars had made a decision, without actually calling a conference to discuss the issues. With the destruction of the Second Temple and the reality of diaspora, the focus of the Jewish people was survival. Tools for survival included a community centered on a synagogue, education, and strictly defined roles for men and women. Men were leaders in the public and religious spheres, and women were wives and mothers, ostensibly leading the private sphere. Anyone who stepped out of line was brought back to reality through community action. Therefore, in a text-oriented religion, women who could serve as "bad" role models had their actions reinterpreted to suit the needs of the survival of a minority group.

So what could they do with an undeniably heroic female figure, namely Judith. she who saved the Jews by beheading the enemy general and managing to escape with his head? The first step was to leave her out of the Tanakh. Esther, that scroll with so many *halakhic* issues in it, was included, but the tale of heroic Judith was not. Could it be that a passive Esther was preferable to an active and aggressive Judith? By placing the story of Judith in the *Apocrypha*, the "External Books," using the excuse that it is post-Prophetic or that there are *halakhic* problems with the text, the scholars were possibly hoping that it would disappear, just as they had hoped that the un-Jewish wedding ring would disappear, and therefore did not discuss it in the Talmud. Judith, too, was not discussed in the Talmud.

But the story of Judith did not disappear. It was referred to in Midrash literature, but more importantly, it was translated into Greek as part of the *Septutagint* project in Alexandria, whose scholars decided to include the *Apocrypha* books. With the rise of the Roman Republic, many Greek-speaking Jews from Alexandria moved to Rome. It may be presumed that they brought the *Septuagint* with them, and that copies were available in the *scuola* (synagogues) as well as in the homes of the very wealthy. The only other keepers of the *Septuagint*, as the Roman Empire turned Christian, were the monasteries.

A legitimate question that one could ask is how many Jews could actually read. The lower classes which initially formed the majority of the Jewish community in the Roman Republic probably could not read the Hebrew letters, since the tombstones that have survived from that time are carved with Greek words. They may have had a basic knowledge of the Greek alphabet and not been totally illiterate. It may be presumed that they learned by listening to texts being read aloud in the *scuola*. The synagogue as a community center for prayer, learning, and assembly was as old as the Second Temple period, and, if the language of the common people was Greek, many texts were probably read in that language. People had prodigious memories in those days, and it may be presumed that exciting narratives were preferred over dry points of law. There are few narratives more exciting that those of Judith and the Maccabees.

The small middle class presumably could read Hebrew, and some members of this group were educated enough to be able to read from the Torah on the Sabbath and to lead prayers. There was no scholarly class yet; that awaited the arrival of the slaves captured by Titus after the destruction of the Second Temple in 70 CE. In the aftermath of the destruction and the founding of the Academy (*Yeshiva*) in Yavneh, the connection between the Jews of Palestine and the Jews of Rome was strengthened.

But despite the growing control of the educated class of rabbis over the Jewish communities of Rome and southern Italy during the period of the Empire, Roman customs developed in an interesting direction. One markedly Roman custom is the reading of *Megillat Antiochus* in the synagogue during the holiday of Hanukah. Roman Jews also eat dairy foods on the holiday to commemorate the heroic story of Judith, who fed salty cheese to Holophernes to arouse his thirst, which would only be slaked by drinking large quantities of wine. They connect Judith's actions with the holiday of Hanukah, but do not mark it with the reading of the Book of Judith. Instead, the story has been reshaped and restructured into a religious poem entitled a *yotzer,* which is a kind of *piyyut,* or pious didactic expression in poetic form. The next question to be addressed is how far back the Judith poem can be traced. If it can only be traced back to the Renaissance, then its revival could be due to Judith's role in Christian Renaissance Italian creativity, which affected the Jewish attitude. If it was earlier than the Renaissance, the *yotzer* would be from a specifically Jewish context. The history of the *yotzer* as a poetic form has its origins in the religious poetry of the Torah, the earliest of which is the victory poem of Moses after crossing the Sea of Reeds. The next outstanding victory poem is that of Deborah after the Israelites defeated the Canaanites. Hymns to God were often composed during the biblical period, and the most outstanding poet whose works survive was David, many of whose creations were collected in the the biblical book known as Psalms.

Poetry was the most popular art form in Middle Eastern general culture, and after the destruction of the Second Temple Jewish religious poetry took the form of the *piyyut*. *Piyyutim* are divided according to their liturgical purposes, differing in their history, structure, and distribution. One of the purposes of the early *piyyut* was to ensure variety in the obligatory prayers, and they were said mainly on Sabbaths and festivals. The oldest and anonymous poets did not use rhyme, instead stressing rhythm and style. One form of this early *piyyut* is the *yotzer*, which enjoyed great circulation in the period between the seventh and eleventh centuries. It is at this time that the Hebrew used moved from the lucid earlier style to a vague, exaggerated, and flowery style, which did not always follow Hebrew grammar; rhyme was the focus now, rather than rhythm. One of the most famous poets of this type of *piyyut* is Eleazar Ha-Kallir, whose religious paeans were composed in the most abstruse Hebrew, either to deliberately make the poem difficult to understand or to allow for multiple interpretations. The mystical nature of the text is trying to depict a level of the language that cannot be put into words; it is supposed to give the language a unique spiritual quality, something that is difficult to articulate in any language. This was the style of the earliest known European examples of the *yotzer*, which were written in southern Italy while it was under Byzantine control. It is to this part of Italy and to this period of time that the *yotzer* of Hanukah points, because it was a center of Jewish life in Italy at that time.

Tracing both the *yotzer* of Hanukah and the inclusion of *Megillat Antiochus* by Italian Jews is difficult, as very few manuscripts have survived from the ancient and early medieval periods. Yet, with the introduction of printing in Italy during the late Renaissance and the appearance of the prayer book in the form of either a *Mahzor* or a *Siddur*, research becomes more feasable. A search through the earliest extant examples of prayer books following Roman custom turns up both the *yotzer* of Hanukah, including the story of Judith and in many cases *Megillat Antiochus,* which is the story of the Maccabees. These did not come out of nowhere, but must have been part of a long tradition. The manuscripts of the early fourteenth-century prayer books that did survive attest to this.

Southern Italy was the confluence of two streams of Jewish intellectual life—that of Palestine and that of an earlier, specifically Roman tradition. The cities of Bari, Oria, and Otranto were loci of bustling Jewish communities which were at once part of the Greek speaking Byzantine world and yet aware of what was going on in the world of Islam, which was spreading across North Africa into Spain in the west, and which was in control of the centers of Jewish religious creativity in the Academies of Baghdad. Closer to home, Sicily was invaded in 827 CE, and southern Italy was subject to attacks from then until 1061. Despite these conquests and reconquests, the Jews in southern Italy flourished.

In his medieval commentary on *Sefer Yetzira*, Shabtai Donnolo, discussed above in Chapter 3, refers to books of the Apocrypha, proving that Italian Jewish scholars read and studied these texts, including the Book of Judith. Book IV in the *Josippon* is a reworking of the *Book of Maccabees*, although it does not make reference to the story of Judith. This too supports the theory that there was a long continuous history of access to the various books of the Apocrypha: the Jews obviously did not need to use the Christian Bible to gain access to their own texts. No matter how open Italian Jews were to the larger culture, sacred texts were beyond the acceptable.

The author of the *yotzer* of Hanukah was Joseph ben Solomon (Yosef ben Shlomo). His name is worked into two acrostics, the first in the final few lines of the first stanza of the poem and the second in the final few lines of the last stanza. It is accepted by scholars that he was from Carcasonne, France, and that he lived before Rashi (1040-1105), who refers to this work in his commentary on Ezekiel XXI, 18. The Jews of the Rhineland originated in Italy, and the poetic styles of the two communities were similar, despite the fact that by the time of Rashi their Talmudic style diverged. We may thus presume that the author, although born in Carcasonne, traveled northward to the more Jewishly populous Rhineland and was either in touch with the southern Italian Jewish communities and their intellectual trends or himself traveled to these centers, something that was quite common then. His identification as "from Carcasonne" was a typical description, probably to differentiate him from other men with similar names. His knowledge of southern Italian poetic styles would also indicate the reverse: that the Jews of southern Italy knew of the poetic creations of the French Jews.

Why did the author use a *midrashic* variant for the Judith story instead of following the story line of the Apocrypha version? Perhaps because *midrash* had an imprimatur of sanctity which the Apocrypha did not, and the creators of religious poetry therefore felt that it was more appropriate to use. But this reasoning only works for France, as in Italy the *Megillat Antiochus* is taken directly from the Apocrypha. Could it be that the Apocrypha narrative was too powerful for the author of the *yotzer*, for Judith is forcefully decapitating the general, and so he preferred the more toned-down version? This would also fit with the fact that the author was

French and not Italian, and French commentators like Rashi were already interpreting biblical texts in a manner that placed women in the preferred diaspora roles referred to above. Yosef ben Shlomo was, it seems, inspired enough by the story to use it in his poem, but only within the boundaries of *midrash*. The Italian Jews incorporated his *yotzer* into their Hanukah service along with their Apocrypha version of *Megillat Antiochus*. They were amenable to this because, as related above, they had a long tradition of connecting the Judith story to Hanukah and seemed to have no difficulty with strong women. They might not have liked the weaker *midrash* variant, but the poem was beautiful, and in the form of *Piyyut* most admired at the time. The Italian Jews made up for the weaker Judith both in their manuscript illuminations and in the *hanukiyyot* that were crafted during the Renaissance, many of which depict Judith with her arms lifted in triumph above her head, holding the sword that was used to behead Holofernes.

The Italian Jews of Renaissance Italy may also have played another role, namely that of spreading the tale of the heroic Jewish Judith to other European Jews who came to northern Italy to have their books printed. The printing process took time, and these Jews stayed in local Jewish communities and were hosted by the wealthier families there. They also went to Italian synagogues and witnessed—if it was Hanukah time—the Italian custom of reading *Megillat Antiochus* as well as the *yotzer*. It may be assumed that discussion of variations in customs ensued, with Italian Jews pulling volumes of the Apocrypha off their bookshelves to share their knowledge. This may well be how the first Yiddish version of the story began. There is no written proof of this method of transmission, but historians surmise it based on what is known. It would be wonderful to find a collection of sermons from that time which could serve as primary source proof. The art of the sermon already existed, and, again, the historian may justifiably surmise that the topic of the heroic Judith was a Hanukah favorite.

Unfortunately, neither the *Megilla* nor the *yotzer* is included in the latest Italian *Siddur*. As both Rabbi Elia Ricchetti of Venice and Rabbi Michele Ascoli of Rome noted, the service had become too long, and in the interest of "streamlining" certain things were dropped. Maybe Italian Jews feel no need for a figure like Judith anymore, but that is not true for the rest of the Jews, for whom the story of the heroic Judith should be part of the school curriculum, discussed in sermons, and included in general knowledge.

Yotzer for Hanukah

In praise of You because you retracted Your anger
And You listened to my prayers, turning your anger against my enemy
And making her like straw in a whirlwind;
I remember and recall the past
And the results of scarlet [acts]
I will tell of the consequences and will not sleep;
I will talk about the sufferings and the vendetta of Antiochus
Who killed my pious and butchered my priests,
When some idiotic people slandered me thus bringing destruction;
After that God gathered horses of fire
Upon which angels rode, angels with swords of fire
So that everybody in the Holy City would see the miracle.

Those arrogant idiots came to slander me
Because of this the king burned with rage
And decided to destroy those who multiplied in Goshen;
The king's rage grew suddenly bigger and bigger
This made me very afraid and threatened my life
I had to hide in the forest like an animal always prowling;
The king decided to destroy and crush the populace
He commanded his general Philippus
To force me to betray my faith and bow to the king's statue.

He ordered who would be made impure with pig
And whose foreskin cut out in a circular form
Whose corpses to throw down, refusing to save anyone;
He let live those who ate abominable idolatrous food
But disheartened those who stayed strong in their integrity
He broke and destroyed those who observed the laws of the Sages;
Two matrons who circumcised their sons
Were hanged by their breasts
And their babies were thrown with their mothers from the tower.

They thought of soiling Eleazar with their sacrifices
But he kept his faith and became even stronger
He rejected with contempt the orders of the cruel tyrant;
Who told him: "I cannot guarantee your life
Unless you will eat your holy meat while pretending to eat unholy meat
I will pretend to believe you so that I can free you."
He [Eleazar] answered crying: "I am ninety years old

And you are asking me to express my belief in God with a lie?
Stop talking to me for I will never change my life."

This righteous one did not betray his principles
And seeing that the old man chose to die rather than betray his faith,
The young men grew ever stronger;
Are You asking for a detailed account of the events
So You will burn with Your wrath the ram and the goat
Striking the head, the feet, the beard, and the neck?
Look and remember all the miseries
That have crippled and disgraced Your community
Will You abandon forever he who became so soiled?

I will now relate the story of the seven
Pious and believing brothers
Who were killed by the tyrant by fire;
Because they refused to eat from his sacrifice
They instead stayed true to He who created the world with His strength
The tyrant hacked apart the first with all his cruelty;
And into a bronze pot full of boiling water
He put the hacked pieces of each limb
And skinned the head with his razor.

The tyrant in his hidden thought
Planned to slaughter his six brothers
Like lambs hanging from hooks;
He thought: I will seduce the seventh, the youngest.
"I will make you rich with gold" he drowsily said,
"And I decided to make you my viceroy."
But the youngest answered immediately.
He shouted: "Kill me, why are you hesitating?
I have no intention of bowing to other gods."

The cruel despot became even more enraged.
He kept hitting the innocent boy
Who grew stronger and enjoyed his suffering.
Their mother saw the sentence against her sons.
And she became so weak over her offspring
That her soul returned to her Creator;
My will is so weak that I have not strength left.
Don't forget those pious people and their slaughter
Be gracious to those who merit it.

He who started all this made another stupid decision:
Those who will not rebel against my edict
and will follow Greek customs shall live;
but those who use their Hebrew names
will be butchered, cut into pieces like a goat
whose carcass is freshly hanging.
He made the ritual waters impure
And the pious ones separated from their wives
But God saw this great suffering and made a miracle.

The Lord who resides in Heaven
Made a source of ritual water for each
Because his pious ones bless him twice daily;
The tyrant then added another horror:
When the bride was to enter the house of her husband
She was first to sleep with the governor;
This was the last straw.
It lasted forty moons and four months,
Until Judah, the holy priest, rebelled.

When the glass was full, God gave charm
To the soon-to-be-married daughter of Yochanan the Hasmonean
Who gathered the people for the wedding feast;
The bride stripped off all of her clothing
And lifted a wineglass to the company
Who lowered their eyes so as not to look at her;
Her brother was in great rage against her
That the honored guests had seen this.
"How could you stand naked before them like a prostitute?"

To him the beautiful young woman replied:
"How dare you rebuke me so hypocritically
when you allow me to lie naked with an uncircumcised heathen?"
Then the spirit of God possessed Judah
And his heart was full of strength and courage.
He prayed and was possessed by an ardent zeal.
He gathered myrtle and spices
As was the custom to do for a wedding
In order to deceive the evil one, pretending to obey his law.

When the Greeks saw from afar the people singing and celebrating
Their leader said—"These important personages
Are finally willing to accept our customs";

He made his armed guards and servants go out
To usher in Matityahu and his sons.
Judah Maccabee drew on his strength;
With the ax used to cut wood he transfixed the adulterer.
He went after the enemy from Acco to Nemerim
Destroying it totally—this was told to Holofernes.

He gathered an army in order to subject Israel;
He encamped one mile off Zion.
My heart was agitated like the forest on the Carmel.
The people returned to their Creator
And everyone lamented, fasted, and cried.
And those more precious than gold meditated on the Torah.
A nobleman, Achior, prophesied to the king,
A nobleman and advisor to dukes and popes,
'They returned to the laws of the Torah and so they
                                                will burn you in the oven.'

When the demon heard this he went into a rage
And ordered that Achior be impaled
at the entrance of the main gate of the city.
He thought, "Tomorrow when I will burn the city
I will use my sword first on the head of that man
Because he said words in favor of my enemies."
But during that night, Judith came to my defense.
Her secret project was blessed and her reasoning excellent.
She encouraged her people and was a torch of fire against Greece.

Content that the city and its citizens were on the right path,
She was very happy and went with her slave,
And putting all of her hope in God
She stopped at the entrance of the enemy encampment
In order to undo their happiness and make them suffer
And feel the punishment for the sins of their leader.
They went to the king to laud her beauty.
"There is not one young woman like her in the entire province."
The king thus wanted to know her and sent for her.

He said: "Tell me where you come from."
She said: "I am from a family of prophets.
I can explain to you things that concern you, my king and master.
Suddenly tomorrow at this time,
Your arms will destroy the city like it was terracotta.

I came here to tell you this news without delay.
When you act within your anger,
Remember your servant
And the young men of my family who will serve in your house."

He whispered: "I will do anything you ask,
If you will do my will, I will elevate you in my house,
As well as elevate your father's family."
She replied: "I am not pure."
So he commanded to let her go, saying:
"Beware not to touch the young woman—she is going to purify herself."
He became like a horse in heat and started to dance.
He gave wine to all his soldiers and made a big party;
He became inebriated and so his neck became the object of a hunt.

Suddenly he fell profoundly asleep.
And his guests murmured that in order to violate the young woman
He lowered his head and is pretending sleep.
They immediately left the tent, each going his way,
They rushed away from their king,
They hurried to their separate tents.
She, the clever one, prayed to God.
She cut off his head like a grain of wheat.
She took it and carried it back to raise the hopes of Israel.

They saw the head but did not believe her.
They ran to the man that he had wanted to impale in his rage
And he answered, "I swear that that is his head."
That night great were the manifestations of joy.
All the pain and sighs disappeared
Because in one moment the persecutor was erased
                                        from the face of the earth.
They danced and celebrated all night
Praising the One who is terrible in his action
But protects His people with great mercy.

When the sun rose there was a great light in the morning.
They prayed to the Almighty and in the luminosity
Declared "Shma Yisrael!"
When the brigands heard the noise of the people,
They thought of awakening the king to prepare a trap,
But they saw him lying dead in his palace.
Their arrogance became humility and their courage dissipated.

They were afraid and pulled out their swords.
Their intended prisoners pursued them and cut them to pieces.

They killed them and made heaping piles of their bodies.
They sang hymns of thanksgiving.
The sages realized the great miracle that happened
And established reading the complete Hallel all eight days
And lighting specific lights each year, forever.
Today Shabbat and Hanukah coincide,
Praise be to You from your nation, still delicate and tender,
And this nation will forever declare that the Kingdom belongs to You.
Your beloved people always search for You
Because You did not stay silent, they exalted You and declared You unique.
Free them from their prison
And they will all pay homage, O Holy One.

Chapter 10

THE LAST CONVERSO

The island of Sardinia lies about 140 miles west of the Italian mainland, and about twice that distance from eastern Spain. While it has about a half-dozen natural harbors, the majority of the coastline is made up of steep cliffs plunging directly into the sea. The harbors themselves lead almost immediately to rocky mountains which make up the majority of the interior. These mountains are almost impassable, and can only be traversed through winding paths that hug the contours of the hills themselves. This geography has contributed to the difficulty that has prevented any invading power from conquering Sardinia. A second factor is the people themselves.

No one knows the origins of the oldest inhabitants of the island. The *nuraghe*, circular multi-storied stone edifices erected without cement, date back about 6,000 years. They are to be found on mountaintops as well as in fertile valleys, and it is presumed that they were the centers of settlements as well as lookout towers which the people used to communicate with each other, especially in cases of invasion.

There are archaeological remnants of Phoenician towns along the coasts, which is logical, since Carthage in North Africa is only about 200 miles away to the south. There are also remnants of Greek towns there. However, it was the Romans who were the first to actually try to conquer the whole island. Roman records testify to the existence of brigands in the interior who consistently attacked Roman garrisons, and also to the fact that the ports were constructed to enable Roman ships to load up with Sardinia's most important export at the time: salt, from the salt mines in the south.

The first historical evidence of the presence of Jews in Sardinia dates back to Emperor Tiberius, who as mentioned in Chapter 2 sent 4,000 young men from the Roman capital to work in the salt mines and fight against brigands. After Tiberius' death, the order was rescinded, but it is unknown how many of these 4,000 Jews returned to the mainland, how many died, and how many married local women and remained on the island.

The next references to Jews in Sardinia date to the period of the spread of Christianity and the establishment of a strong center in Rome. Pope Gregory the Great (530-601 CE) acted upon the forced seizure of synagogues by some zealous Christians on the island, demanding that they be returned to the Jews, attesting not only to their presence but also to their importance.

The island was under Byzantine control, was invaded by Arabs from North Africa, and was then subjected to the rivalry between Genoa and Pisa before it was taken over by Catalan and Aragon in 1323. Along with this last group of invaders came a small group of Spanish or Sephardic Jews, probably merchants looking for new markets. They settled along Sardinia's west coast, mainly in the cities of Sassari and Alghero, but some came to the much smaller city of Bosa, to the south of the other two. While life in Spain was acceptable for Jews in the fourteenth century, as the Reconquista moved relentlessly southward there were some Jews who were looking for better opportunities elsewhere. Word probably spread about the economic opportunities available in Sardinia, and in municipal records we can find the appearance of Jewish artisans, who joined the wealthier merchants and the first loan bankers. The artisans came with their special capabilities and knowledge, especially in the fields of dyeing, leatherworking, and silversmithing. Sardinia was a perfect place for the dyeing industry to flourish, as one of the main products of the island is wool from its millions of sheep, raised by most of the people of the interior. These sheep also provided hides for the workers to turn into excellent quality leather, which could then be exported by the merchants.

Jewish merchants, often in partnership with non-Jews, exported salt, semolina, pasta, orzo, wheat, cheese, and skins. They imported, mainly from southern Italy, linen, hemp, cotton, tuna, rice, almonds, figs, and saffron. From Flanders they brought in corduroy and lace.

The Jews of Catalan and Aragon were personally protected by their kings in their new location, as *servi cameri*, just as they were in Iberia. This was one factor contributing to the growth of the Sardinian Jewish communities. A second factor was the fact that during the fourteenth century, Jews were expelled from France, including Provence (1316, 1339), and were attacked in both Germany and Austria, leading to an infusion of Jews from these locations into the Catalan/Aragon mix in Sardinia.

As in Spain, the Jews followed an *aljama* structure of self-government with three representatives, who were annually elected and confirmed by the royal local representative, and worked to administer the community. The representatives came from the top stratum of rich merchants and doctors, and they were advised by an elected council of eight to ten men. There was a chief rabbi for each community, as well as a Bet Din, or religious court. Controlling all, as representative of the king, was the *Rav de la Corte*, or court's rabbi.

Things began to change in Sardinia in the fifteenth century, as the anti-Jewish legislation of Spain was applied to the island as well. Laws passed in 1412 initiated special clothing for Jews, to be followed by anti-usury laws in 1447. By the 1480s, the Jews were forced into a *Juderia*, segregated from Christian markets, forbidden to wear gold jewelry, and taxed for kosher slaughtering. The *Juderia* of Cagliari, which held about 1200 Jews, is the easiest to trace, and was right next to the walls of the city, near one of the towers, next to Santa Croche church. The synagogue, fountain, well, oven, and abbatoir are now part of the University of Cagliari, as is the church. A similar thing happened in Alghero, and the synagogue, built in 1381, was eventually taken over by the church.

The final anti-Jewish act in Spanish Sardinia took place in 1492, when King Ferdinand and Queen Isabella used their combined forces to reconquer the entirety of Spain and expel all non-Christians from their domain. The Spanish Expulsion included the overseas provinces of Sicily and Sardinia. The Jews of Sardinia chose to either leave their island, heading for the Kingdom of Naples, North Africa, or the Ottoman Empire, or convert, keep their Judaism secret, and hope that the edict against them would be rescinded as so many others had been in Jewish history.

It is within this context that we can follow the route taken by one family which chose to convert but remain secret Jews. The name *De Riu*, translated as "of the river," is a common type of last name for Jews, whose names are often connected to a geographic place (such as Ancona), a profession (such as Goldsmith), or a paternal origin (such as Abramson). The river in question could very well be the river Temo, which flows down from the mountains of central Sardinia to the sea, ending at Bosa, providing the only navigable river of the island.

The Jewish community in Bosa appears to have consisted of about a hundred people, too small to warrant the construction of a synagogue. They probably met for services in the home of one of the wealthiest community members, much as Jews in small communities have done throughout the ages. It can be presumed that they had kosher meat, bread, and cheese, as well as kosher wine for sacramental purposes. A school for the children would have been directed by a tutor, or a part time teacher, and then—according to their social class—the children would have learned the family business or craft.

Along the southern bank of the river, across from the main town, is a collection of houses that were inhabited by dyers, wool workers, and leather workers, three fields in which the Jews were well represented. The setting is perfect for these crafts, as the water there is plentiful and clean. The homes of the other Jews were probably closer to the *duomo*, on the northern side of the river, possibly on the narrow Via Santa Croce, which is lined with five-story buildings, or the poorer streets further up the hill leading to the protective castle.

Due to their economic endeavors, the Jews knew the interior of the island as well as the coast. It was logical, then, for them to move up into the mountains in an attempt to escape the long arm of the Inquisition as the Spanish government started to strictly enforce its anti-Jewish laws. Heresy was punishable with death, and everyone knew who the converts were.

The members of the De Riu family probably moved up the mountains gradually, searching for a town in which they would feel safe. The town in which they finally settled was Sedilo, which is built along a mountain ridge. With a population of about 300 people, it was large enough for artisans to earn a living, yet small enough to escape the notice of the central power. The oldest standing church there, Santa Croce, dates to the fourteenth century and holds about fifty worshippers in its oldest section; it was expanded about a century later to hold about 300. It is possible that Sedilo was chosen because its annual three-day July festival, the *Ardia*, ensured that customers would come and would be open to buying things like baked goods, silver trinkets, and anything that could be connected to the town's patron saint, San Costantino.

The Converso family moved into the area near the church, as was typical for Jews in their circumstances, and the *Carrela e sos Ebreos*, the Street of the Jews, is a block away. It is only about one hundred meters long and six meters across, and consists of about eighteen to twenty one- to two-story houses, each with a small garden in the back. It seems from the street's name that the townspeople knew that the De Rius were Jews, and didn't care.

How long the De Rius continued to be merchants is unknown. The only luxury item that they continued to deal in was lace from Flanders. What can be seen is that many family members gradually bought land—something that they could not do as Jews—and began raising the same kinds of crops as their neighbors did. They raised flax, which they turned into linen, grapes which they turned into wine, wheat for bread, and sheep for meat, wool, and cheese. They continued silversmithing and probably dyeing fabrics, as well as leather-working.

What became of their secret Jewish identity? How long could it last?

Maria Maddalena De Riu was born on February 29, 1876, in Sedilo, to Costantino De Riu and Maria Lodde, and died there on May 22, 1960. She married Giovanni Battista Lodde, a relative, and gave birth about every two years for decades, but only eight of her children reached adulthood. She was the last of the real Conversos.

The most obvious Jewish thing that Maria Maddalena did was light candles every Friday night, in a cabinet that was recessed into the wall and could be closed should any stranger enter the house. A couple of her grandsons remember this well. They also attest to the grand housecleaning she performed every spring before Passover/Easter, accompanied by the whitewashing of all of the walls, a custom observed by Sephardic Jews in many parts of the world. There was no issue over the baking of *matza*, as one of the Sardinian breads, known as *zikki*, is in fact *matza*. There were also absolutely no Christian images in her home. Anyone who has visited Sardinian homes knows how incredible this is, for every room in every house is likely to have a Mary or a Jesus in it, often with multiple crosses and icons.

The main church in Sedilo, built to hold hundreds of worshippers, is constructed in the typical rectangular shape with various chapels along the right and left sides. The entrance is facing the front of the church, and when you enter you face the altar all the way up in the front. Maria Maddalena always entered the church—when she went—through a side door at the right of the altar, which led into a small chapel which most of the congregants could not see into from the main nave. She always came late, often escorted by one of her grandsons, sat perched at the edge of her seat during the service, and rushed out before the end so as not to have to participate in the Eucharist, eating the wafer. She never crossed herself, neither in church nor out of it. There were never any pork products in her home. She used to sprinkle salt on bread at the beginning of a meal and make a blessing over the bread in Sardinian.

Maria Maddalena was knowledgeable in herbs, which was common among Jews, and knew how to discern between good and poisonous mushrooms. She was also a kind of folk healer, and people would come to her for help when they were sick. She would put a mixture of herbs into a bowl, add water, mix in three pieces of rock salt, and would softly chant unrecognizable words while passing her fingertips around the rim of the bowl. Jews tended to be well versed in both medicine and pharmacology over the centuries, and this could be a remnant of this knowledge. When former patients were asked if the herbal concoctions worked, the response was in the affirmative, some of the time. In a village where the local trained doctor would prescribe two aspirin for everything from gout to cancer, the people usually resorted to the traditional healer for help.

As is the case in many other countries, one of the sources of information on a Jewish or Converso community is the cemetery. In Sedilo there are two sections in the cemetery, the main section, in which graves often have elaborate tombstones, and the front edge, where people were buried directly into the ground without even fancy coffins. After a number of years, the bones of these "outsiders" would be exhumed and placed in a community ossuary. Therefore, there is no tombstone for Maria Maddalena. But she was definitely an "outsider," as was her husband.

When Maria Maddalena died, as far as anyone could remember, she was surrounded by her family. No priest was allowed in, and so she did not have extreme unction, the final Christian sacrament.

Why do I define her as the "last" Converso? Because even though some of her children and grandchildren continued some of the "strange" things that she did, they didn't know why they were doing them. The education of Conversos usually followed the female line, but none of her three daughters received this education. Not only that, but toward the end of World War II, when the news of Nazi atrocities and the huge number of dead Jews reached Sardinia, Maria Maddalena would go around sighing, "What is the point? What is the point?" No one understood the reference, and just thought that it was one more strange thing said by a strange woman. But within the context of a Converso's life, this complaint makes sense, for she was asking what was the point of trying to continue as a Jew, if this was the result.

What Maria Maddalena could not have known, for she died in 1960, was that one of her granddaughters would get a job in the Italian consulate in Jerusalem, meet a Moroccan Jew, convert to Judaism, and raise three Israeli children, all of whom served in the Israel Defense Forces. She could not have known that a favorite grandson would follow an intellectual and spiritual journey from Catholicism to Judaism, and would convert in Israel, marry an American Orthodox Jew, and raise two daughters educated in the American Modern Orthodox school system.

The rest of her family is totally Christian, with only some of the older members aware of and interested in their unique family history. There are no Conversos left in Sardinia.

Street sign in Sedilo, Sardinia. Italian (new) name above original
Sardinian name *Carrela e sos Ebreos*—Street of the Jews
(Photograph, R. Fodde collection)

Bose, port on western coast of Sardinia, meeting Temo River. Four building
on the right were for Jewish craftsmen who were leather workers and dyers
(Photograph, R. Fodde collection)

CONCLUSION

The story of Jews in Italy is one of re-creation and tenacious resistance to merging with the larger community. It is a story of economic creativity and of people locating niches for themselves when there were adverse laws limiting how they could earn a living, and it is the story of expansion when they were treated well. It is a story of intellectual creativity in the realm of Jewish thought, literature, and poetry, and in the larger world of the Italians. While Jews were divided into potentially divisive social strata—in which the upper class had more in common with their non-Jewish counterparts than with poorer Jews—the glue of the community continued to keep them all bound together.

We can trace the formation of Italian Jews back to ancient Rome, as the community arrived from Alexandria and a destroyed Jerusalem. These two cities illustrate the push and pull of emigration, as the Jews of Alexandria moved voluntarily for economic reasons, and the Jews of Jerusalem arrived involuntarily, as conquered slaves. It is from this kernel that the Jewish community evolved, with its own customs and its own identity. As the centuries passed, this core group was reinforced by the arrival of other small Jewish groups, such as those from Provence or Germany, who kept their own customs for a while but tended to merge with the larger Italian group as time passed. It was not until the arrival of the Sephardic Jews, some of whom immigrated as early as the fourteenth century, but most of whom came after 1492, that a distinct Jewish group kept its own identity alongside the Italian group. In the unique example of the newly-developed city of Livorno, only Sephardic Jews, in their multiple guises, were permitted to settle. Yet they too gradually became Italian.

After the efflorescence of the Renaissance, with its creativity and relative tolerance, Italian regions began to either expel their Jews—for example from the islands of Sicily and Sardinia, as well as from the south of the country—or confine them in what became known as the *ghetto*. The Papal States emptied its Jews into the two ghettos of Rome and Ancona, while papal pressure on the rulers of northern regions forced them to gradually follow suit. The only large city to escape this was Livorno.

Crowded together into an intolerable space, the Jews turned inward and found spiritual consolation as well as community support. Relief came in the form of the new ideas of the French Revolution, as well as in the form of the French armies tearing down the gates and walls of the *ghettos*. Fired up by the new nationalism, Jews joined the liberating forces and participated actively in the unification of a new and modern Italy. By this time the definition of "Italian," which had been evolving over the centuries from its original form, which referred to shared history, language, religion, and culture—including music, art, and cuisine, had replaced "religion" with the modern concept of "nationalism."

Proudly Italian and proudly Jewish, the Italian Jews expressed their modern identity in the large, elaborate new synagogues they constructed in Rome, Trieste, Milan, Turin, Livorno, and Florence. The new architecture reflected their modern identity. When the First World War broke out, they joined the Italian forces, many ending up as decorated heroes. But then the unimaginable occurred: after the successful rise of Fascism in the years following the war, Mussolini partnered with Hitler and anti-Semitic laws were enacted demarcating the Jews as unequal Italians. But Italy was not Germany, nor was it Poland. While there were roundups of Jews and some deportations to death camps, the majority of Italy's Jews survived World War II. Even so, the shock of their treatment caused many to lose faith in their country and their future in it.

Post-war Italy saw the arrival of new groups of Jews. Some were Ashkenazi survivors of the Holocaust who were housed in Italy until documents arrived to allow them to re-locate to the United States, Canada, or Latin America. Some headed for British Mandated Palestine. A small number stayed on. Larger groups arrived from Libya as a result of political upheavals, and their number was supplemented by Jews who left Iran and Lebanon for similar reasons. Jews leaving the Soviet Union were often temporarily housed in Italy; some of them stayed as well.

While these new groups initially stayed separate from the Italian Jewish community, set up their own synagogues and community facilities, and followed their own customs, they are gradually becoming Italian, just as other Jews arriving in Italy over the millennia became Italian. We do not know what shape this new Italian Jewish community will take in the future, but considering how tenacious Italian Jews have been, we can predict that it will be both very Italian and very Jewish.

Appendix

MAPS

The Mediterranean of Ancient Rome

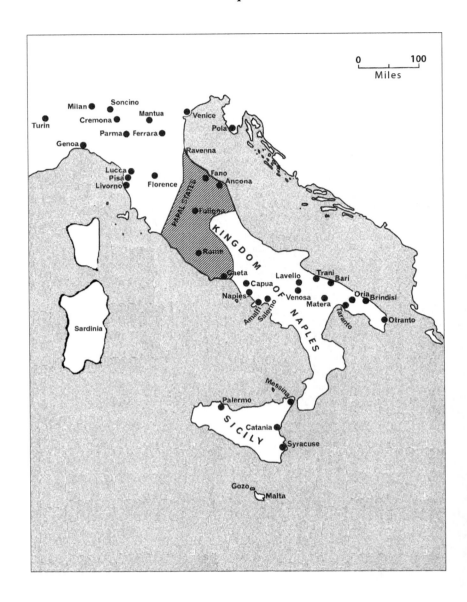

Southern Italy and Sicily

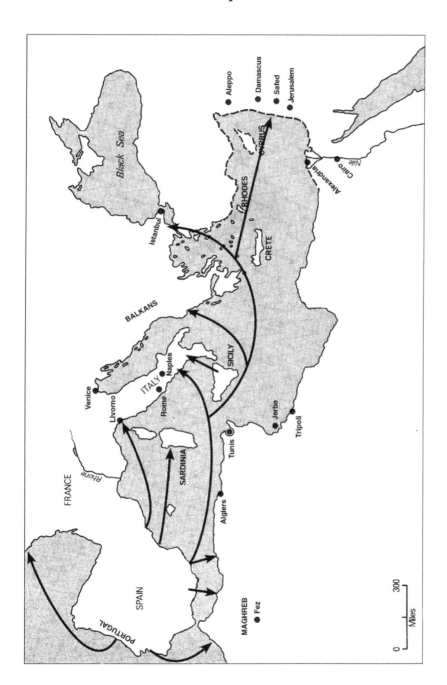

Expulsion from Spain and Portugal, 1492/7

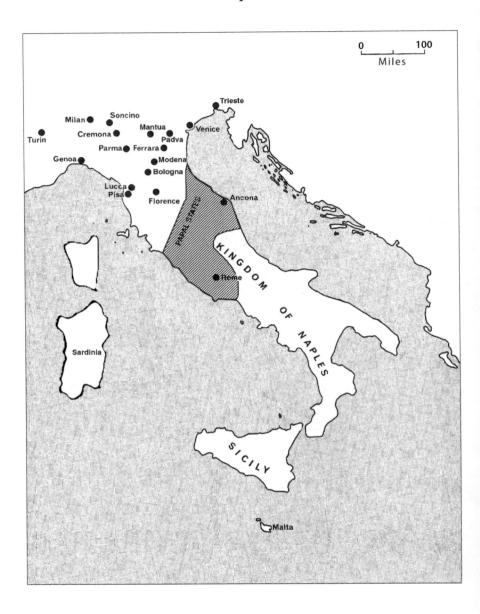

Ghettos of Italy, 16th Century

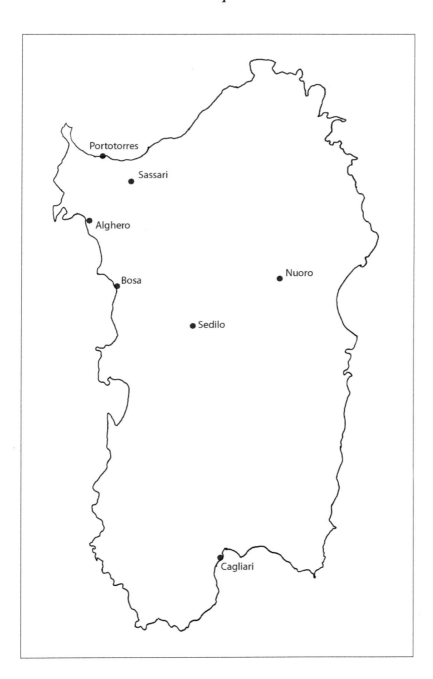

Sardinia

Index